BY ROYAL COMMAND

BARNUM IN EUROPE

Steve Ward, PhD
Modern Vaudeville Press

By Royal Command: Barnum in Europe / Steve Ward

Edited by Thom Wall

Cover photo adapted from: *Barnum's American Museum illustrated*, 1850. (Library of Congress)

Cover typography by Robin Gunney

Modern Vaudeville Press
113 E. Mayland St.
Philadelphia, PA 19144
USA

www.modernvaudevillepress.com
info@modernvaudevillepress.com

ISBN (print): 978-1-958604-26-7
ISBN (ebook): 978-1-958604-27-4
Library of Congress: 2024925949

BY ROYAL COMMAND:

BARNUM IN EUROPE

To Humbugs everywhere.

CONTENTS

ACKNOWLEDGEMENTS

In compiling this book, I have received help and support from many people. I would especially like to mention the following;

The staff of the National Fairground and Circus Archive, Sheffield; the Leeds Library; Kathleen Maher and Daryn Reman-Lock of the Barnum Museum, Bridgeport, Connecticut; Thom Wall; The Royal Archives at Windsor Castle; the staff at the British Library, Boston Spa; and of course, Linda my long-suffering circus-widow wife, who is my constant support and encouragement.

FOREWORD – KATHLEEN MAHER

History is an endless sea of wonder, with each discovery pulling you deeper into its depths. I will admit, I did not seek out P.T. Barnum ... I stumbled onto him ... and there was no going back.

Firmly rooted in 19th-century American social and cultural history, I (like so many) overlooked one of the most impactful figures who shaped culture and entertainment as we know it today. A powerhouse of innovation and ambition, Barnum transformed the way we engage with amusement; he opened the doors to all who sought the delights of theatrical enjoyment, popularizing the idea that entertainment was a respectable endeavor and could be both a spectacle and an educational experience. Barnum broke down barriers, making the arts accessible to people from all walks of life, regardless of class or background. Barnum revolutionized the concept of mass entertainment, bringing together diverse audiences to marvel at the extraordinary and the wondrous. His genius lay not only in his ability to promote and captivate, but also in his understanding of human curiosity, and using it to create experiences that transcended mere amusement and speak to deeper cultural narratives. In doing so, he laid the foundation for modern entertainment by blending awe, education, and inclusivity in ways that continue to influence the industry today.

When we think of Barnum, we tend to think of the circus—an image that conjures visions of dazzling performances under the Big Top—but there is so much more to his legacy. In truth, the circus was Barnum's *retirement project.* He was over 61 years old when he launched *The Greatest Show on Earth* in 1872, and he was a well-established international brand. Barnum's lesser known but equally extraordinary stories of struggle and triumph came with the creation of *Barnum's American Museum* on lower Broadway in New York in 1842. And so, begins the remarkable story of *By Royal Command*...

Using primary source accounts written by Barnum himself, *By Royal Command* illuminates a pivotal time in history that set the trajectory of modern entertainment...the international introduction of Charles Stratton (aka General Tom Thumb). Born in Bridgeport, Connecticut in 1838, Charles, a young boy just over two feet in height, was a natural-born entertainer and catapulted into stardom at five years old at Barnum's American Museum. Notably, he was the first "child star" who quickly became an international sensation. What unfolds in *By Royal Command* is not fiction, but rather the captivating true story of how Barnum, with his natural gift for showmanship and marketing, turned Charles into one of the earliest global entertainment celebrities. The 1844-1847 European tour of General Tom Thumb was one of P.T. Barnum's most defining achievements, elevating both his career and Stratton's to unprecedented heights while redefining the nature of popular entertainment.

By Royal Command will take you on an unforgettable journey with Barnum and Charles. From Buckingham Palace to the courts of Europe, General Tom Thumb enchanted all who had the good fortune to see him perform, and the royal endorsements immediately elevated Barnum's troupe to the heights of European society, garnering international headlines and attracting aristocrats, statesmen, and royalty across the continent. What followed was a whirlwind tour that made

Tom Thumb a household name and a towering figure in the public imagination, forever changing the landscape of popular culture and entertainment history.

Many thanks to historian, author and fellow 'Circademic' Steve Ward. *By Royal Command* is a 'must read' for all those fascinated by the origins of modern entertainment and the extraordinary figures who shaped it. With rich historical detail and firsthand accounts, By Royal Command offers a captivating glimpse into the world of 19th-century showmanship, celebrity culture, and the power of human curiosity. This book is an essential read for history enthusiasts, entertainment scholars, and anyone who wants to explore the remarkable journey of P.T. Barnum and General Tom Thumb, whose legacy continues to influence the entertainment industry today.

Enjoy!

Kathleen Maher
Executive Director, Barnum Museum
Bridgeport, Connecticut, USA

FOREWORD – STEVE WARD

I was a bit of a prankster when I was young. There was nothing I liked better than playing a practical joke on people. My Grandfather would often say to me 'You're a bit of a Barnum, you are!' I didn't really know who Barnum was at that time but I understood that he was someone who would easily fool people. That appealed to me—someone who could become famous just by fooling people.

As I grew older, I became fascinated by the stories that I read about the man; how he could persuade people to believe that what they were seeing was what he wanted them to see. Exhibitions of a rather terrifying skeleton with the head of an animal and the body of a fish were supposed to portray a mermaid; a seemingly ancient 160-year-old black woman was promoted as the nursemaid to George Washington. All of these were, of course, hoaxes or 'humbugs', as the press termed them. One particular story stuck in my mind, particularly as I am interested in words. It was how Barnum, on seeing the crowds gathered in his American Museum and wanting them to move through quickly, placed a sign saying 'This way to the egress'. Enthusiastic people flocked to see the 'egress', only to find themselves out on the street; *egress* being another word for *exit*. But rather than being angered by the experience, many people were amused at the way they had been tricked.

As my interest and involvement with circus developed, I was aware of the Barnum and Bailey circus but I didn't immediately make the connection between Barnum the 'King of Humbug' and Barnum the circus proprietor. Understanding came at a later age. In fact, I suppose that my knowledge of Barnum was as much as any other person; he was the 'king of humbug', he had a museum in America where he exhibited all things weird and wonderful, and he ran a circus.

It was much later that I learned that Barnum was a very complex individual driven by ambition, a need for approbation, and a desire for wealth. His professional life was phrenetic and his private life somewhat turbulent. He embarked on grand schemes, sought royal approval, and made and lost a fortune—only to rebuild himself. He was a figure of renown and it was his three-year tour of Great Britain and Europe, with his dwarf protégé General Tom Thumb, that catapulted him to international fame.

Whatever your knowledge of Phineas T. Barnum, I hope that *By Royal Command* will be of interest and offer an insight into how that visit shaped his life for the future.

Steve Ward
Leeds

P T Barnum c.1855 (Library of Congress)

INTRODUCTION

Barnum—everyone seems to know the name of Phineas Taylor Barnum, no matter what age they are. Much of this is down to popular imagery of the man as portrayed in the film *The Greatest Showman*[1] or the Broadway musical *Barnum*[2]. Ask who Barnum was and you will get a variety of responses, such as a con-man, a humbug, a showman, a circus owner. Well, he certainly was a showman and, in much later life, a circus owner. And he was a self-confessed humbug, defining a humbug as;

> A genuine humbug consists in making a man feel that he has got the worth of his money, that he has seen wonders such as could not be found elsewhere on the face of the earth – that these wonders must have cost the 'enterprising & liberal proprietor' many sleepless nights & oceans of gold – and that in fact in truth the beholder of the humbug is much indebted to the owner thereof for having kindly permitted him (by paying for it) to behold this precious sight whatever it may be (Letter #138 11 September 1845)[3]

Very few people who fell for Barnum's humbugs actually felt that they had been unscrupulously 'conned' because Barnum always gave them something for their money—even if it was not exactly what they had expected! There is a fine line between being a con-man and a humbug and Barnum always seemed to lean towards the humbug.

Barnum was more than this. He was a very complex character, driven by the need to be a success at whatever he set his mind to, and a need for approbation. He was full of restless ambition. Throughout his life he was many things in addition to the above; a newspaper publisher, a museum owner, an author, a politician, a philanthropist, and an entrepreneur with interests in several and various schemes. In his lifetime he made a fortune and then managed to lose it in a single failed project—only to rebuild himself to become one of the wealthiest men in America. But Barnum also had a darker side. He exhibited people of non-white ethnic backgrounds as 'curiosities' for profit. In the same way, he exhibited those who were physically different; people who suffered from dwarfism, giantism, or hirsutism for example. In a speech he made at a time when running for Congress, Barnum exhibited the enslaved and admitted to owning slaves himself—and worse;

> I did more – I whipped my slaves. I ought to have been whipped a thousand times for this myself, but by then I was a Democrat – one of those non-descript Democrats who are northern men with southern principles[4]

These racist attitudes stretched to his American Museum. A report given in the *Coleraine Chronicle* gives an example;

> An English Baronet arrived in New York with a favourite black servant who had been in the family for many years ... The next day he mounted the steps of Barnum's Museum with the design of inspecting the curiosities of that establishment; and here again he was refused admission unless he left his servant at the door. As he could not, of course he had to turn back (*Coleraine Chronicle* 13 November 1847)

It could also be argued that Barnum's importation and exhibition of exotic animals, birds, and fish in what we would deem today as being inappropriate and unsuitable conditions, displayed further cruelty driven by the desire for profit. However, nineteenth century attitudes were very different from today and it is easy for us to criticise with hindsight. For many, Barnum's exhibitions were as educational as they were entertaining, and we should not let our modern-day sensitivities detract from that. We may not like aspects of our history, but history is not necessarily to be liked, but learned from.

Although Barnum was becoming a household name in America by 1843, it was his later tour of Britain and continental Europe from 1844 to 1847 that cemented his name as an international celebrity. It is difficult to write about this tour without also taking into consideration his prize protégé Charles Stratton, otherwise professionally known as General Tom Thumb. Barnum relentlessly exhibited this dwarf child performer throughout the tour and he would not have achieved his international fame without Tom Thumb—and Tom Thumb would not have achieved his success without Barnum. Although their financial contractual arrangements may have changed during the tour, in reality one would not, perhaps even could not, have existed without the other.

Barnum chose the epithet 'Tom Thumb' for his miniature exhibit with good reason. The character was well known in British folklore. The earliest record of the name "Tom Thumb" was in a published work of 1621 by Richard Johnson, *The History of Tom Thumb*[5], although the name and story may have existed before this date in oral history. The name appears in the folk cultures of many other European countries, such as in France as *Le Petit Poucet*[6] and in Germany as *Der Kleine Däumling*[7]. Tom Thumb also appears in dramatic works such as Henry Fielding's 1730 play of the same name and in the work *Hop o'My Thumb*, later adapted by Albert Smith specifically for General Tom Thumb.

The story of Tom Thumb follows the pattern of a 'swallow' cycle, where the main character is swallowed by a succession of animals and people, situations from which Tom always emerges triumphant. In Johnson's story, Tom Thumb, a fairy child no larger than his father's thumb, is swallowed in succession by a cow, a raven, a giant, a fish, and a miller (after an exploit at the court of the legendary King Arthur). In between, he made his appearance from a bag of cherry stones, a pudding, a fish dish presented to King Arthur, a walnut shell, a bowl of frumenty,[8] a snail shell, and a mouse trap. Barnum must have been aware of the story because several of the above devices—particularly the appearances—were adapted for use in General Tom Thumb's performances.

Charles Stratton was, by his own admission, 'one of nature's freaks'[9], though we should be careful as to how we interpret his use of the term. It is not necessarily a negative or pejorative word; that very much depends upon its usage. Sherman[10] makes a case that the term *freak* is

COMING OUT OF SALT-BOX.

Tom Thumb coming out of a salt box (Illustrated London News *21 March 1846*)

a slur when applied to a person with disabilities and that the associated term of 'freak show' merely propagates that slur. But historically, the term implied a difference or 'otherness', and that embraced those with genetically physical differences such as dwarfism, giantism, conjoined twins, etc—or even the self-created different, such as the tattooed man—or even the ethnically different.

> The freak show was billed as entertaining and educational, offering the opportunity to learn about the mysteries of the body and the 'realities' of people from foreign lands. No surprise, then, that men of medicine and science, along with ethnologists and anthropologists, flocked to the shows: a potpourri of the peculiar served up as respectable, theatrical, titillating and spectacular.[11]

In dealing with historical records and materials they are very often written in the language of the time. Throughout this work, the terms *freak* and *dwarf* are used in their historical context and no offense is intended by the author. Barnum tapped into this nineteenth century fascination with the different and his exhibitions were the forerunner of his later travelling shows that accompanied the Barnum & Bailey circus[12].

This book is not a definitive history of the life of P. T. Barnum. It is intended as a celebration of his life, particularly of the time he spent in Europe and of his contribution to the cultural fabric of British society. I hope it will be of value to those with a specific interest in the man as well as to the curiosity of the general reader. Whatever you know, or think you may know, about P. T. Barnum this book will be revealing.

Advertising for Barnum's American Museum c.1860 (Library of Congress)

Notes

1   *The Greatest Showman*. 2017. 20th Century Fox.

2   *Barnum!* 1980. Bramble/Stewart/Coleman. Broadway Musical.

3   *P. T. Barnum Copybook 1845 – 1846*. Barnum Museum. Connecticut Digital Archive Collection.

4   *The Dark side of P. T. Barnum*. 2022. Youtube online at https://www.youtube.com/watch?v=7Vnlp4vlcU

5   Altemus, H. (ed.) 1999 *The History of Tom Thumb*. (From 1621 manuscript) The Project Gutenberg. Online at https://gutenberg.org/cache/epub/1988/pg1988-images.html

6   Perrault, C. (1697) *Histoires ou Conte du temps passé*. One of eight fairy tales published in this volume

7   Grimm, brothers. 1819. *Grimm's Fairy Tales*.

8   A form of porridge in medieval cuisine.

9   *Pictorial Times*. 13 March 1847.

10 Sherman, H. (2014) 'Freak' is a slur and 'Freak Show' is propagating it. Disabled people deserve better. *The Guardian*. 26 September 2014.

11 Woolf, J. (2019) *The Greatest Show on Earth? The Myths of the Victorian Freak Show*. BBC History Revealed. November 2019 issue. Online at The Myths Of The Victorian Freak Show. HistoryExtra

12 Saxon, A. H. (ed.) (1983) *Selected Letters of P. T. Barnum*. Columbia University Press pxv

CHAPTER 1 – BECOMING A SHOWMAN

Phineas Taylor Barnum was born on the 5th of July 1810 in the small township of Bethel, Connecticut, some 30 kilometres northwest of Bridgeport. It was a time of great turmoil, for although America and Britain were not officially 'at war' there had been acts of aggression on both sides from as early as 1807. The British naval vessel off the coast of Virginia, *HMS Leopard*, demanded that the American ship the *Chesapeake* return some deserters who had signed on that vessel. The demand was refused, and the British ship opened fire on the *Chesapeake*, causing so much damage that she had to be brought to a stop. The British boarded her and the men were taken. This caused President Thomas Jefferson to create the embargo of 1807, ceasing trade with Britain and France, and to calling up 100,000 militia in the event of a full-scale war. Small scale naval conflicts continued, notably with the American warship *President* severely damaging the smaller British vessel *The Little Belt* and killing several of the crew. The Americans also believed that the British were secretly supplying weapons to the indigenous native population of Canada. Thereby gaining their support with the promise to restore all lands in the American Midwest to them. Tensions between America and Britain grew to the point where war was officially declared on June 18th, 1812, when Barnum was almost two years old. The war would rage backwards and forwards across America for the next three years, from Niagara in the north to Florida in the south, where America was in conflict with Spain. Battles were won and lost on both sides, the British even marched into Washington and set fire to the White House,

The Capture of the City of Washington (Library of Congress)

destroying many public buildings. Such was the outrage at the British being in the capital that President James Madison issued a proclamation to the nation, leading with this opening paragraph;

> Whereas the enemy by a sudden incursion have succeeded in invading the capital of the nation, defended at the moment by troops less numerous than their own, and almost entirely of the militia; during their possession of which, though for a single day only, they wantonly destroyed the public edifices, having no relation in their structure to operations of war, nor used at the time for military annoyance; some of these edifices being also monuments of taste and of the arts, and others repositories of the public archives, not only precious to the nation as the memorials of its ORIGIN and its early transactions, but interesting to ALL nations, as contributions to the general stock of historical instruction and political science. [Dated 1st September 1814] (*The Times* 20 October 1814)

The President then went on to exhort all Americans to come together 'in a manful and universal determination to chastise and expel the invader'. And all this was happening at a time when Britain and America were in negotiations for a peaceful end to the war! Indeed, a treaty was signed by both parties in the Belgian town of Ghent on Christmas Eve 1814. Unfortunately, it took some time before word of this treaty actually arrived in America. Several further battles took place, with a notable defeat for the British at the battle of New Orleans in January, and the Treaty was finally ratified by Congress on February the 16th 1815. The war officially came to an end.

Initially the Federalist governments in the New England states, of which Barnum's native Connecticut was one, were generally opposed to the war feeling that beneficial trade routes were becoming a war zone and would impact on their economies. At the outbreak of war, Connecticut refused to mobilise its militia for the campaign. The Connecticut General Assembly condemned the war and stated that 'It must not be forgotten that ... Connecticut is a FREE, SOVEREIGN and INDEPENDENT State; and that the United States is a confederacy of states ...'[1] Although opposed to the war, Connecticut did see some localised action. The British blockaded the port of New London in December 1813 and in April 1814 a British force landed in Essex and torched or captured several ships. In the summer of 1814, the British decided to blockade the entire New England coast in an effort to extinguish any commercial trade from those states. An attempted assault on Stonington that August was repulsed by the local populace supported by some of the state militia. Although these actions may have softened public attitudes towards the war, Federalist representatives from Connecticut, Rhode Island, Vermont, and New Hampshire held secret discussions at the Old

State House in Hartford, Connecticut. The Hartford Convention, as it became known, considered secession from the United States. They called upon the central government to protect [the states of] New England and to provide financial aid to their battered economy. Unfortunately, the timing was wrong. By the time that the Convention had issued its declaration on January 5th, 1815, Britain and America had signed the peace treaty and the war had officially ended.

Growing up in this unsettled atmosphere, I feel sure that Barnum must have been aware of some of the tensions of the time, although in his autobiography (Barnum, 1855) he makes no mention of it whatsoever;

> I must pass by the first seven years of my life ... I commenced going
> to school at the age of about six years. The first date which I recollect
> inscribing upon my writing book was 1818.

His paternal grandfather Phineas Taylor, after whom he was named, was a landowner and a justice of the peace and would have been more than interested in the problems of that time. Barnum was very close to his grandfather. Did he shield him from all of this, or did he tell him tales of war and peace? Being as close to his grandfather as he was, I feel sure that Phineas Taylor would have taken time to explain the ways of the troubled world to his first grandchild. I find it interesting that Barnum never mentions this, as it may have held some significance in his later considerations of a visit to Britain.

By all accounts Phineas Taylor was a consummate practical joker and a lover of money; for a while he ran his own lottery. Both of these traits seem to have been passed on to Barnum from an early age, especially the thrill of making money.

Before I was five years of age I began to accumulate pennies and sixpennies. At the age of six years my grandfather informed me that all my little pieces of coin amounted to one dollar, and if I would go with him and take my money, he would show me something worth having. Placing all my wealth in a pocket handkerchief which was closely wound up and firmly grasped, I started with my grandfather. He took me to the village tavern ... The landlord took my deposits and presently handed me a silver dollar. Never have I seen the time (nor shall I ever again) when I felt so rich ...

Clearly this had a huge effect upon the young child and the acquisition of money was something that underpinned most of Barnum's ventures throughout his life. As a young boy he continued to save his pennies and then began making money on 'holidays' by producing and selling candy. He was never a child who liked working on his father's farm, preferring to dream up his own money-making schemes. By the age of 12, he had saved enough money to buy a sheep and a calf, thinking himself 'a man of substance'. He also made his first visit to New York in his twelfth year. A local farmer was driving a herd of cattle to market and needed a young boy to assist him. They would be gone for about one week. This was a great opportunity and adventure for Barnum. New York was *the* great metropolis and many people in rural Connecticut at this time would never get the opportunity to visit such a great city. Accordingly, the next day he set off for the city with a dollar in his pocket that had been given to him by his mother. He planned to use the money wisely and make profit. He began by haggling and bartering over sweets and toys, such things as young boys were interested in. But, like many would-be entrepreneurs, he learned the hard lesson of loss and soon his one dollar (and any profits) were gone. He had to resort to finally 'trading' his handkerchiefs and a pair of stockings to feed his desire for molasses candy! Returning home at the end of his adventurous week he had nothing to show for it and was roundly chastised for his missing laundry. He had learned a serious lesson.

Barnum had an aversion to the hard work of farming life, so his father set him up as a store clerk selling dry goods, groceries and other sundries that the local people needed. The store operated on a cash, credit, and barter system and people paid for goods with such things as butter, beeswax, axes, corn, and other such things that they might have surplus to requirement. Always seeing the opportunity, Barnum soon branched out into buying and selling candy and, with a good line in patter, was soon persuading the local mothers to buy candy for their children.

At the age of 15, Barnum's father died at the relatively young age of 48. He left little provision for his wife and family; in fact, his estate was declared insolvent. Barnum had no choice but to continue working as a store clerk, although by now he had moved to a small village a mile or so north of Bethel. It was here that he embarked upon a lottery scheme, taking after his grandfather. It was also perhaps the first great 'deception' that he played on the public. He devised the scheme so that there was one grand prize of $25, 50 prizes of $5 each, 100 prizes at $1, 100 prizes at 50c, and 300 prizes at 25c. He had 1000 tickets printed and sold them at 50c per ticket. Here was the clever catch that he devised. Instead of prizes being in cash, winners received goods to the value of that prize, and the goods were always surplus stock in the store. In a previous transaction he had obtained many empty glass bottles which he had to move on, and all prizes included a few, or many in some cases, of these. In this scheme he also realised the power of advertising. The lottery was promoted as follows;

MAGNIFICENT LOTTERY! $25 FOR ONLY 50CTS!! OVER
550 PRIZES!!! ONLY 1000 TICKETS!!!!

Soon he had sold all of the tickets and when the prize draw took place people left with arms and baskets full of sundry goods, some of which, I am sure, they did not necessarily want.

> A young lady who had drawn five dollars would find herself entitled to a piece of tape, a spool of cotton, a paper of pins, sixteen tin skimmers, cups, and nutmeg graters, and a few dozen glass bottles of various sizes!

When asked if he would exchange the glass and tinware for other (more useful) goods, Barnum refused, stating that it would be against the rules of the lottery. In this way he netted $500 in cash against an outlay of

*A Trade in Bottles (*Cassell's Illustrated Family Paper *7 February 1855)*

goods that nowhere near matched that sum. Although many of the winners were disgruntled at their prizes, many saw the funny side of how they had been duped into parting with their money. Barnum had not told any lies; he had just been a little creative with the truth; something that he would perfect throughout his life.

By 1828, Barnum had opened up his own retail confectionary and fruit store in Bethel, with the help of his grandfather. He had offered Barnum, rent free, one half of his carriage house in which to establish the business. As well as making a good profit in his store, he was also still running a lottery scheme. Overall, this gave him a substantial income and enough to support a wife and, in the summer of 1829, he married a local girl named Charity Hallett. His lottery scheme continued to grow, with the appropriate advertising that he was now so fond of, that he opened up an office in the nearby township of Danbury as well as branches in Norwalk, Stamford and Middletown. He had amassed enough income to buy three acres of land in Bethel from his grandfather in 1830 and to have a house constructed on the land for him and his

wife. By the age of 20 he was married and had become a successful entrepreneur, with a good income and property.

Prompted by an outbreak of religious fervour in Connecticut and wider New

Portrait of Charity Hallett Barnum
c.1847 by Frederick R Spencer
(Barnum Museum, Bridgeport,
Connecticut)

England during 1831, Barnum was concerned that the formation of a 'Christian Party in politics' would allow religious fanatics to have too much influence. Accordingly, he decided to establish his own newspaper so that he could write editorials against such a move. He bought a printing press and in October 1831, the first edition of the weekly newspaper *The Herald of Freedom* was published. It was widely distributed throughout Connecticut and also in the states of Rhode Island, New York, and Ohio. With a degree of naivety, Barnum left himself open to accusations of libel through the material he published. Three times during his three-year tenure as editor he was taken to court, the last occasion resulting in a fine of $100 and imprisonment for sixty days. While he was imprisoned in Danbury he was well catered for. His cell was well furnished, he was allowed to receive visitors, and he continued to edit his newspaper. His status within the community had grown to the extent that when he was released there was much celebration. His release was covered in his own newspaper on December the 12th, 1832[2];

TRIUMPH OF THE PEOPLE

On Wednesday last (the 5th inst.) P. T. Barnum, the editor of this paper, was liberated from the Common Jail in Danbury, where he had been doomed during the last *sixty days*, by order of the Hon. David Daggett, for an alleged libel on Mr. Seth Scelye. The friends of civil and religious liberty ... began to flock into the town by hundreds, at an early hour of the day. Twelve o'clock was the hour appointed for the delivery of the Oration and before 11 o'clock, A. M. the Court-House was literally crowded to overflowing, and many hundreds were obliged to remain outside of the house, in consequence of the great number of people present. The number of persons present on this interesting occasion is estimated at

FIFTEEN HUNDRED ... At sunrise the National Standard was hoisted and continued to wave beautifully and triumphantly throughout the day. A national salute was fired at 9 o'clock. At half-past eleven o'clock the Committee of Arrangements waited on Mr. Barnum at the Jail, with a request for him to accompany them to the Court-House. The service commenced at 12 o'clock ...

An especially commissioned ode was then sung, after which a series of toasts were made, twelve in all. The toast to Barnum was the final one;

12 – *The Editor of the Herald of Freedom* – The fearless advocate of truth and liberal principles – a faithful Sentinel on the ramparts of Freedom – a terror to Bigots and Tyrants – a young man just on the threshold of active life, whom neither bolts nor bars nor prison-walls can intimidate or drive from the path of honour, truth, and justice.

After the singing of *Home, Sweet Home!* there was a lengthy ovation after which Barnum rose to reply to the toast. It was a lengthy response, only part of which I give here.

My Fellow Citizens – I can find no language to express what I feel on looking about me and observing so great a concourse of friends ... It is but little more than one year since first I undertook the arduous and expensive task of publishing a periodical, the columns of which should be free and accessible to all sects and parties, with a view to let reason, God's best gift to man, determine who was right and who was wrong. You cannot but be aware my friends, with whom and with what I have had to contend during the last year. You all know that I have grappled with the lion in his den; I have been obliged to contend with all the 'pride, pomp, and circumstance' of power, popularity, and wealth; with error, ignorance, and superstition; and with that which is worse than all these combined – the *hydra-headed* and powerful monster, PRIESTHOOD ... The voluntary and deafening acclamations ... amply repay me an hundred-fold for all the unhappiness I ever experienced in being torn from the sweet embraces of a family and friends, and incarcerated in a gloomy dungeon; and they serve as an incentive which spurs me onward in the glorious cause of intellectual emancipation, with the determination never to shrink from doing my duty as a sentinel upon the watchtower of liberty.

Barnum clearly had the gift of oratory and could 'turn a good phrase' when necessary. It is interesting to note that in the above he makes particular reference to his publishing venture being 'expensive' as well as arduous. Was this really necessary to state? And his 'incarceration in a gloomy dungeon' is certainly something of an exaggeration of the truth of the situation. Barnum gives coverage of the event in his autobiography;

P. T. Barnum and the band of music took their seats in a coach drawn by six horses, which had been prepared for the occasion. The coach was preceded by forty horsemen, and a marshal, bearing the national standard. Immediately in the rear of the coach was the carriage of the Orator and the President of the day, followed by the Committee of the Arrangements and sixty carriages of citizens, which joined in escorting the editor to his home in Bethel. When the procession commenced its march amidst the roar of cannon, three cheers were given by several hundred citizens who did not join in the procession. The band of music continued to play a variety of national airs until their arrival in Bethel (a distance of three miles), when they struck up the beautiful and appropriate tune of 'Home, Sweet Home!' After giving three hearty cheers, the procession returned to Danbury. The utmost harmony and unanimity of feeling prevailed throughout the day, and we are happy to add that no accident occurred to mar the festivities of the occasion.

It must be remembered that this piece was probably written by Barnum himself, certainly he edited it, and to what extent he exaggerated the occasion we will not know. What is certain is that he was using the media to self-promote and to raise his level of celebrity within the community. Far from being a criminal, he was now a celebrity and a martyr to the cause of free speech. One might have expected that, with his status within the community, he might have continued towards an illustrious career as a newspaper editor; but not so. Barnum's restless spirit was always seeking bigger and better options. His retail business did not thrive as well as he would have liked and in 1831, he had sold out the business to Horace Fairchild. By 1834, *The Herald of Freedom* had moved its publishing base to Norwalk, CT and was edited by his brother-in-law, John Amerman. The following year it was sold to George Taylor. Barnum was now left with no business concerns and therefore no income. Although he had made a significant amount of money through his business ventures, he had frittered most of it away, as he explained;

> I had learned that I could make money rapidly and in large sums, whenever I set about it with a will, and I did not hesitate to expend it in various extravagances as freely as I gained it ... To be sure, I thought that at some future time I should begin to accumulate by saving, but I cared not for the present, and hence I scattered my means with an open and unsparing hand.

He therefore decided to move his family to New York City in the winter of 1834 to seek his fortune. But he found that fortune was not easy or immediate to come by. He took on several temporary jobs during those first few months in New York City. None of them paid well but adequate to keep his wife and baby daughter Caroline, born in 1833, alive while he continued to look for that golden opportunity. In the spring of 1835, he received some debts owed to him to the value of several hundred dollars. With no other work available, he decided to open a boarding house and then bought a small share in a local grocery store. Always at the back of his mind was the ambition to have his own exhibition and he had already responded to an advertisement from Scudder's American Museum for the purchase of a 'Hydro-oxygen Microscope' but found the outlay required far beyond his means. Then, in July 1835, he read the following;

CURIOSITY – The citizens of Philadelphia and its vicinity have an opportunity of witnessing at the MASONIC HALL, one of the greatest natural curiosities ever witnessed, viz., JOICE HETH, a negress aged 161 years, who formerly belonged to the father of Gen. Washington. She has been a member of the Baptist Church one hundred and sixteen years, and can rehearse many hymns, and sing them according to former custom. She was born near the old Potomac River in Virginia and has for ninety or one hundred years lived in Paris, Kentucky, with the Bowling family. All who have seen this extraordinary woman are satisfied of the truth of the account of her age. The evidence of the Bowling family, which is respectable, is strong, but the original bill of sale of Augustine Washington, in his own handwriting and other evidence which the proprietor has in his possession, will satisfy even the most incredulous (*The Pennsylvania Inquirer* 15 July 1835)

This piqued Barnum's interest, and he immediately went to Philadelphia to view this 'curiosity'. Having viewed Joice Heth, of whom he gives a lengthy description in his autobiography, he asked her 'owner', R. W. Lindsay, for further proof of her age. Barnum was shown the 'original' bill of sale, yellow and faded and in a glass frame. It was purported to be dated the 5th of February 1727 and appeared to be fully signed and sealed by George Washington's father. Barnum was satisfied with this provenance and immediately fell into discussion with Lindsay as to the possible sale of Heth. Lindsay appears to have been ready to sell his interest in Heth and a sum of $1000 was agreed, of which Barnum only had $500 at the time. Returning to New York he sold his share of the grocery business to his partner to raise the necessary capital. The articles of agreement for the sale of Joice Heth to Barnum were completed on the 6th of August 1835. The full document is given in his autobiography. Barnum was now, in his own words, the proprietor of his first exhibit. He chose to use the term "proprietor" rather than "owner" as the ownership of enslaved peoples was becoming a contentious issue in the United States and was already illegal in some northern states by this time. In later life, Barnum became a strong Abolitionist and found his association with Heth a somewhat embarrassing event. As he wrote in his memoir of 1869[3], the episode was;

> The least deserving of all my efforts in the show line was the one which introduced me to the business ... a scheme in no sense of my own devising, one which had been sometime before the public and which had so many vouchers for its genuiness that at the time of taking possession of it I honestly believed it to be genuine ...

Although there is an air of apology in this statement, he does not elucidate on why the Heth episode was the 'least deserving' of his efforts. At no point in the memoir does he deny that he bought Heth nor does he have any forthright misgivings about it. This is one of the darker aspects of Barnum that we see after the first exhibition of Joice Heth, in that he was quite content to exploit others for financial gain. Did he care for her or was she just another commodity to him? Already in an advanced stage of ageing, Washington (2006) claims that Barnum had some of her teeth removed to make her appear even older.

Contracting Lindsay to oversee the exhibition of Heth in Philadelphia, Barnum travelled to New York to find a suitable venue for his first real major exhibition. What better place than Niblo's Theatre, a pre-eminent place of entertainment on Broadway and Crosby Street? William Niblo, the owner, agreed with Barnum to exhibit Heth in a large apartment in his own nearby house. Niblo would be responsible for furnishing the apartment and the lighting, printing costs, advertising, and ticket sales and would keep one half of the total receipts. This amounted to $1500 per week of the exhibition. Knowing the value of good publicity, Barnum commissioned Levi Lyman to write a brief memoir of Heth which was sold to visitors at 6 cents per copy, entitled *The Life of Joice Heth. The Nurse of George Washington*[4]. Lyman had been engaged by Barnum as an assistant in exhibiting Heth. Barnum also had a woodcut portrait of Heth printed and circulated on small bills and posters.

One of the major selling points of Heth, in addition to her advanced age of 161 years, was that she had reputedly been a nursemaid to George Washington. At this time in the nineteenth century, Washington was seen as the greatest American of all times; he was the 'Father of the Country'. To see the person who had, as Barnum wrote,' put clothes on the unconscious infant who was destined in after days to lead our heroic fathers to glory, to victory, and to freedom' was a must for many people. Visitors flocked to the exhibition and the event was covered in many newspapers, even in Britain, although quite low key and matter of fact;

> NEGRO LONGEVITY – A female negro slave, of the name of Joyce Heth, is now exhibiting in this city, who had attained the extraordinary age of 161 years. A visit which we paid her yesterday has removed whatever doubts we previously entertained as to the facts confirmatory of this extraordinary instance of longevity – *Pittsburgh (United States) Advertiser* (*Sun (London)* 27 August 1835)

Barnum then took Heth on a frantic seven-month long tour of the northeastern states, visiting towns such as Providence, Boston, Newark, Albany, New Haven, Springfield, Hartford, and several others. He exhibited her 'in taverns, inns, museums, railway houses, and concert halls'[5] Wright (2018) maintains that he exhibited her for six days per week and up to 12 hours a day. Always ready to pull a publicity stunt to improve audience figures, when in Boston he found that ticket sales were waning, an 'anonymous' letter appeared in the local press claiming that Heth was nothing more than an automaton. This prompted even more people to visit his exhibition to see for themselves! It must have been a gruelling time for the aged Heth, even if she was not the claimed 161 years old. Before enthusiastic audiences, Barnum would begin the exhibition by recounting the story of Joice Heth before reading the framed bill of sale. He would then lead a question-and-answer session and the whole was rounded off with Heth singing a few hymns. The vast majority of people believed what they were told and what they

THE GREATEST
Natural & National
CURIOSITY
IN THE WORLD.

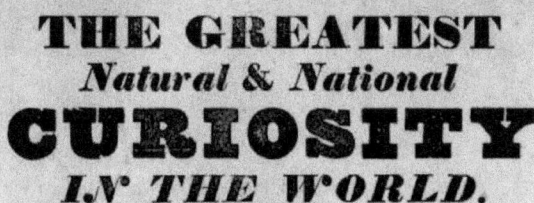

Nurse to GEN. GEORGE WASHINGTON, (the Father of our Country,)
WILL BE SEEN AT

Barnum's Hotel, Bridgeport,

On FRIDAY, and SATURDAY, the 11th. & 12th days
of December, DAY and EVENING.

JOICE HETH is unquestionably the most astonishing and interesting curiosity in the
World! She was the slave of Augustine Washington, (the father of Gen. Washington,)
and was the first person who put clothes on the unconscious infant, who, in after days, led
our heroic fathers on to glory, to victory, and freedom. To use her own language when
speaking of the illustrious Father of his Country, "she raised him." JOICE HETH
was born in the year 1674, and has, consequently, now arrived at the astonishing

AGE OF 161 YEARS.

She Weighs but FORTY-SIX POUNDS, and yet is very cheerful and interesting. She
retains her faculties in an unparalleled degree, converses freely, sings numerous hymns,
relates many interesting anecdotes of *the boy* Washington, and often laughs heartily at her
own remarks, or those of the spectators, Her health is perfectly good, and her appearance
very neat. She is a baptist and takes great pleasure in conversing with ministers and religious persons. The appearance of this marvellous relic of antiquity strikes the beholder with
amazement, and convinces him that his eyes are resting on the oldest specimen of mor-
tality they ever before beheld. Original, authentic, and indisputable documents accompanying her prove, however astonishing the fact may appear, that JOICE HETH is in
every respect the person she is represented.
The most eminent physicians and intelligent men in Cincinnati, Philadelphia, New-
York, Boston, and other places, have examined this *living skeleton* and the documents accompanying her, and all, *invariably,* pronounce her to be, as represented, 161 *years of age!*
A female is in continual attendance, and will give every attention to the ladies who visit
this relic of by-gone ages.
She has been visited in Philadelphia, New-York, Boston, &c., by more than
TWENTY THOUSAND Ladies and Gentlemen, within the last three months.

Hours of Exhibition, from 9 A. M. to 1 P. M. and from 3 to 5, and 6½ to 10 P. M.

ADMITTANCE 25 Cents, CHILDREN HALF-PRICE.

Printed by J. BOOTH & SON, 147, Fulton-st N. Y.

Poster for Joice Heth exhibition c.1836 (Library of Congress)

saw. Opinions about the ethics of displaying a human being for public voyeurism were divided, however, even in Britain;

> We here saw, still living, the very woman who nursed his infancy; and she has worn the chain and badge of slavery from that hour to the present time. Britons blushed for America, and were oppressed with a thickness of the very heart to think that, for more than one hundred years after the infant hero had been pillowed in the bosom of this stranger, Joyce Heth should have remained a slave. We were ready to ask, when we visited her, where are the sensibilities of a people who can tolerate so gross an outrage upon every soft and holy feeling, as to allow this living mummy, this breathing corpse, to be dragged through the country, exhibited to the idle gaze of strangers, and often exposed to the rude offensive merriment of thoughtless youth? ... During many months she has been conveyed from place to place as the last sands of life were thus running out, and more had been gained than the sum for which Washington's father sold her in 1727 (*Morning Herald (London)* 3 June 1836).

Heth died in Bethel on February the 19th 1836; Barnum was at home in New York. That he viewed her little more than a commodity is shown by this comment in his autobiography;

> I shed tears upon her humble grave – not of sorrow for her decease, but of regret on account of having lost a valuable and profitable curiosity.

Her body was conveyed to the city and Barnum engaged the services of Dr Rogers, a prominent surgeon to carry out a post-mortem examination. The ultimate indignity imposed on this aged woman by

Barnum was that he allegedly sold 1,500 viewing tickets at 50 cents each for people to watch her examination. The *New York Sun* of February 26th 1836 reported on the post-mortem in some detail;

> The anatomical examination of the body of Joice Heth yesterday at the City Saloon, resulted in the exposure of one of the most precious humbugs that ever was imposed upon a credulous community. We were somewhat surprised that a public dissection of this kind should have been proposed, and were half inclined to question the propriety of the scientific curiosity which prompted it ... [here follows a lengthy detailed report of the dissection and examination of the body] ... From these evidences ... it seemed to be the unanimous opinion of all the medical gentlemen present, that Joice Heth could not have been more than *seventy-five*, or, at the utmost, *eighty years of age!* ... We believe, however, that the person who exhibited her in this city is not inculpated in the deception, but that they took her at a high price on the warranty of others. Still, it is probable that $10,000 have been made by this, the most precious humbug of modern times.

The popular press, the 'penny newspapers', labelled this a 'humbug' and a giant hoax. Barnum's name was now truly associated with this term and established him a showman of some merit. It matters little as to whether he actually believed in the truth of Joice Heth or not, it was the way in which he enthusiastically 'sold' the idea to the American public that was the turning point for his career. As Lindfors (1987) wrote;

> Barnum thus began his career in show business by going into debt to buy a superannuated female slave, who turned out to be a fraud.

The life of a showman clearly appealed to Barnum because while he was exhibiting Joice Heth in Albany he came across an Italian juggler and acrobat. Impressed by the man's juggling and balancing abilities he engaged Signor Antonio, as he was then billed, to work for him at a rate of $12 a week plus travel and lodging, with the proviso that Barnum could exhibit him anywhere within the United States for 12 months. He also insisted that Antonio change his name to Signor Vivalla, as it sounded more 'foreign'. Barnum arranged for performances in New York and Washington.

Towards the end of a bitterly cold January in 1836 Barnum and Vivalla were in Philadelphia at the well-known Walnut Theatre. During the second night's performance Barnum was disturbed to hear hissing coming from a section of the audience. He managed to trace the source of the disturbance and found it was a circus performer by the name of Roberts, who claimed that he could do anything that Vivalla had done, and more. Barnum saw his opportunity. He immediately printed cards that issued the challenge that Vivalla would pay $1,000 to anyone who could replicate his acts. Roberts accepted the challenge but in a private meeting with Barnum he confessed that there were things that he could not do that Vivalla could but that there were other things he could do that Vivalla could not. Realising that he could not easily win Vivalla's wager he accepted Barnum's offer to be engaged that night for $30, under Barnum's specific direction. Barnum then put the two men together to secretly rehearse their contest, with Vivalla being the winner but with Roberts showcasing his skills. In the meantime, Barnum set about his publicity machine, with press coverage and handbills that ensure the competition night was a sellout.

Barnum records that the total receipts for that one night came to $593.25, of which he received $197.75. The competition over, Roberts accepted defeat but challenged Vivalla to another contest at a place and time of his choosing for a wager of $500. The crowd roared their approval on both sides, but it was not publicly known that Barnum had further engaged Roberts for one month to perform as he directed. The rematch took place the following week and then further trials of skill between the two took place in several other towns during the month. They were all staged events under Barnum's direction but, even if the crowds were aware of this, they enthusiastically embraced the entertainment. As he observed;

> The entertainment of the time may be an offset to the 'humbug' of the transaction ... for the public appears disposed to be amused even when they are conscious of being deceived.

Joice Heth having died, Barnum was now left with Vivalla as his main source of income. He arranged with a travelling circus proprietor, Aron Turner, to engage Vivalla with his company for the summer. Barnum would receive payment for Vivalla's services, but he would also be responsible for paying Vivalla's wages. This balanced out neatly and Barnum's only profit would be a 20% share of the total profits of the company. Barnum toured with the circus throughout the summer acting as ticket seller, secretary, and treasurer. They toured widely, by horse and wagon, and the experiences gave Barnum a good grounding in the life of a travelling showman. Vivalla left the company in May 1837 to travel to Cuba where he would perform on his own account. Having spent a year as a travelling showman, Barnum felt the need to return to New York and to a more settled life.

Looking for business opportunities to ensure a more stable life for his family, Barnum embarked upon a mercantile partnership with a German who was a manufacturer of waterproof paste for leather, paste blacking, cologne water, and bear's grease. Barnum was responsible for the accounts and sales. For several months he appeared quite content with his new way of life but the showman within him kept calling. By the spring of 1840, he had hired a saloon in the New York Vauxhall Gardens. Here he presented a company of singers, dancers, and variety entertainers. It was not a huge success and he closed his production at the venue in the August. But now he was left with no income yet again, so what next? He engaged a company of variety entertainers and took his show on the road. There were financial ups and downs during the seven-month long tour and he returned, almost broke, to New York in April 1841. He vowed never to be a travelling showman ever again!

Small time jobs came and went, and he was even tempted to lease the Vauxhall Gardens saloon again for a short season in the summer of 1841, turning over a profit of around $200. He could not stay away from show business. It was shortly after this that he saw that Scudder's American Museum building and collection was for sale. Earlier in his career, Barnum had wanted to purchase some exhibits from Scudder's Museum. Now he was in a position to explore the possibility of buying the whole outfit. The asking price was $15,000, well beyond Barnum's means. Undaunted, he approached Francis Olmsted, a wealthy retired merchant, and asked if he would consider purchasing the museum on Barnum's behalf. He would then repay the loan from the success that he was sure the museum would be. Olmsted was naturally wary but was impressed by Barnum's enthusiasm and impeccable references. The only stumbling block was that Barnum had no unmortgaged land that he could offer as security for the transaction. But then he remembered that his grandfather had gifted him some land on his birth. In reality, the piece of land known as Ivy Island was little more than a swamp, but Olmsted was not to know this. Accepting this land at face value secured the transaction for Barnum. Olmsted agreed to fund the project. In discussion with the vendor, Barnum had managed to barter his way down to $12,000 and Olmsted agreed to a 10-year lease on the property. On the morning that the papers were due to be signed, the vendor withdrew from the sale, stating that he had sold the museum and collection to another museum named Peale's Museum Company at a higher price—and that they had already paid a $1,000 deposit against the sale.

Barnum was devastated but did not give up. He discovered that the buyers were a speculative group of investors. With all his editorial experience. Barnum coerced some newspaper friends of his to allow him to mount a campaign against potential shareholders in the company. So efficient was this that the proposed sale of shares fell through, and the company would forfeit the deposit paid if the balance due was not paid on time. Of course, with the failure to sell shares there was no way the company could raise that balance. Barnum had planned this and had already met with the vendor to reach agreement that if the balance was not paid on time, then the museum would be sold to him. This is what happened and on the 27th of December 1841, Barnum officially took ownership of the American Museum.

Barnum's American Museum, as it was renamed, opened in January 1842 six days a week and 12 hours a day—all for the princely entrance price of 25 cents. It was a five-storey building that offered many varying attractions, from a working model of Niagara Falls to an aerial garden (though that garden was just two tubs with withered plants!) It was a place of information and entertainment, of scientific knowledge and dreamed up fantasies, and a place of cruel voyeurism. It was an immediate success and people flocked to pass through the doors to view the exhibitions; the physical and the mechanical, the natural and the unnatural.

One of the earlier exhibits that excited interest was what Barnum called 'The Feejee Mermaid'. If Barnum claimed that he genuinely believed in the age of Joice Heth, this exhibit was a definite 'humbug' inflicted upon the people. Contrary to popular belief, Barnum did not make, or cause to have made, the mermaid himself but he was responsible for 'selling' it to the masses. Sometime in the summer of 1842, the manager of the Boston Museum, Moses Kimball, brought the exhibit to the attention of Barnum. Being taken with the idea of exhibiting this strange specimen, Barnum decided to hire it and exhibit it under his own name. In fact, the 'mermaid' had been in existence for some time and had even been exhibited in London as early as 1822;

THE MERMAID – A mermaid, if we are to place implicit credit in the present appearance of the figure, is now exhibiting in St James's-street. The head is the size of a baboon's, and is thinly covered with strong black hair; the nose bears a close resemblance to the human form, so likewise do the chin, lips, fingers, nails, and teeth, which are full and perfect. The resemblance to the human form ceases immediately under the breast, and beneath them are placed two horizontal fins; then comes the mermaid's tail, exactly that of the salmon species – this part of the body is quite scaly, and furnished with six fins. The height of the animal is rather more than two feet; it is shrivelled and dried like a mummy ... The present proprietor, it is said, obtained the animal in Batavia [present day

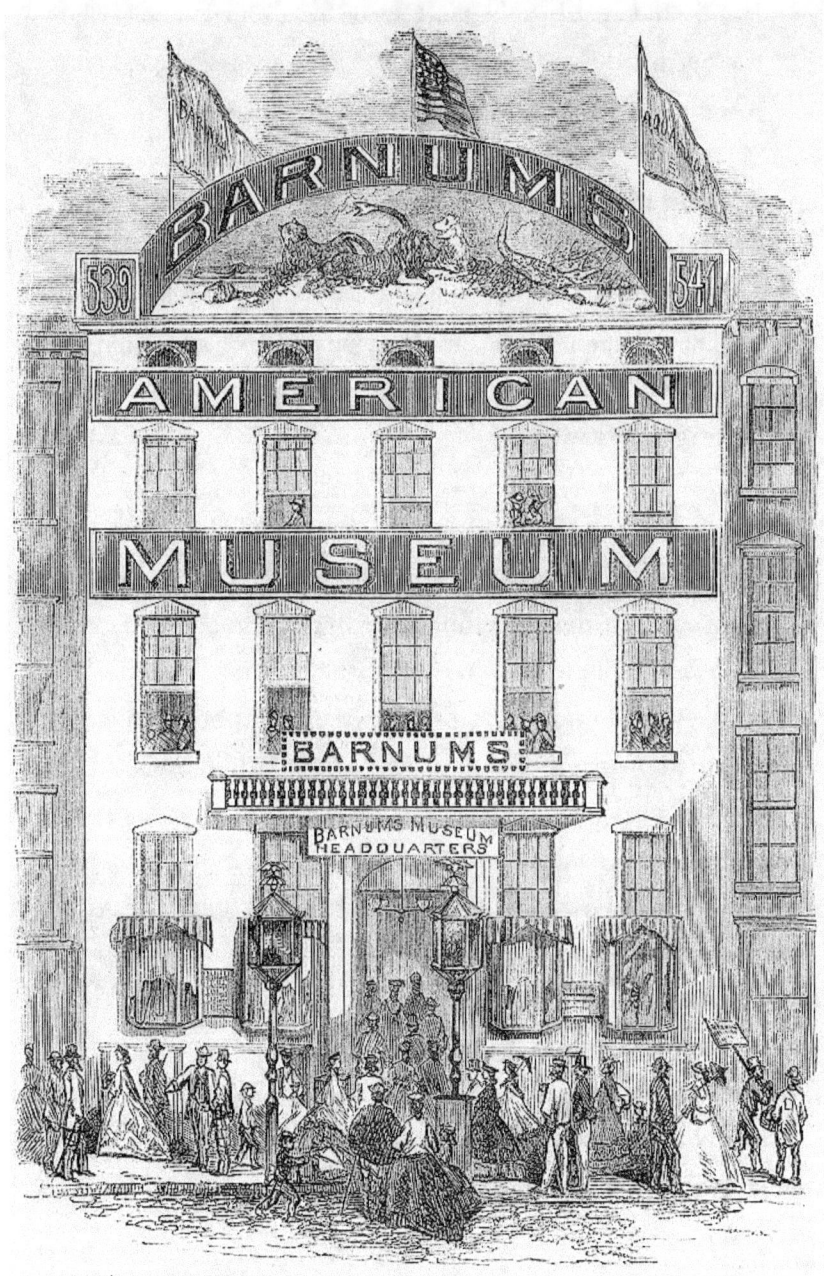

BARNUM'S NEW AMERICAN MUSEUM, NO. 539 & 541 BROADWAY, N. Y., BETWEEN SPRING AND PRINCE STREETS.

Barnum's American Museum 1864 (Library of Congress)

Jakarta, Indonesia], from the Captain of a Dutch vessel, who had purchased it in China – it was then in its present condition (*Commercial Chronicle (London)* 26 October 1822)

Even Barnum admitted;

The animal was an ugly, dried-up, black-looking, and diminutive specimen, about three feet long. Its mouth was open, its tail turned over, and its arms thrown up, giving it the appearance of having died in great agony.

A far cry from the voluptuous female figure with the tail of a fish as portrayed in popular mythology! Barnum realised this, acknowledging that the mermaid had been manufactured, and set about his deceptions. Firstly, he had a colleague of his impersonate a learned gentleman, Dr Griffin, from the London Lyceum of Natural History who was to be the purported owner of the mermaid. Neither Griffin nor the Lyceum actually existed. Griffin strategically showed the exhibit to a small number of people to arouse interest. Then Barnum released letters to three different newspapers anonymously, giving information about the mermaid being in New York. At the same time, he prepared some 10,000 leaflets with information about mermaids (which would be sold at one penny each) and commissioned some woodcuts of voluptuous mermaids that he released to the newspapers. Mermaid fever began to take hold in New York, and people clamoured to see this strange creature, which was initially displayed at the Concert Hall at 25 cents admission.

The mermaid caught near the Feejee Islands and now exhibiting, for three days only, at the Concert Hall, 406 Broadway, is creating a wonderful excitement, thousand daily visiting it. A committee of scientific gentlemen yesterday examined it, and not only pronounced it genuine, but decidedly the greatest wonder in the world. It positively cannot be seen after Saturday of this week. (*New York Daily Tribune* 11 August 1842)

The exhibit then moved to Barnum's American Museum. To Barnum, it was not important as to whether people believed that they were going to see a real mermaid but that they believed that they *might* see a real creature. With careful planning and clever publicity Barnum had sold the popular imagery of a mermaid and created a 'must see' event—even if the actual exhibit little resembled that image. With Griffin's eloquent discourse on mermaids, people were ready to believe that this mummified object *could have been* at one time what they had hoped to see. Most visitors were satisfied with this, even if some newspapers were more dismissive—but all good publicity!

> IMPORTANT TO NATURALISTS – A MERMAID CAUGHT ... A mermaid we have seen! Not in the alluring garb and seductive form represented in the picture books, with an Angel's face ... the mermaid we saw has none of these attractions, but is as ugly a little monster as ever seen, resembling more in appearance, about the upper part of the body, a *mummified* monkey, than an angelic fish. Still, the monster is one of the greatest curiosities of the day ... (*Southport Telegraph* 24 August 1842)

The Feejee Mermaid was a great draw for Barnum's Museum. In the four weeks before the exhibition the receipts had been $1272 but at the end of the exhibition this had risen to $33,411.93; Barnum had almost tripled his income during the exhibition period. After exhibiting at the

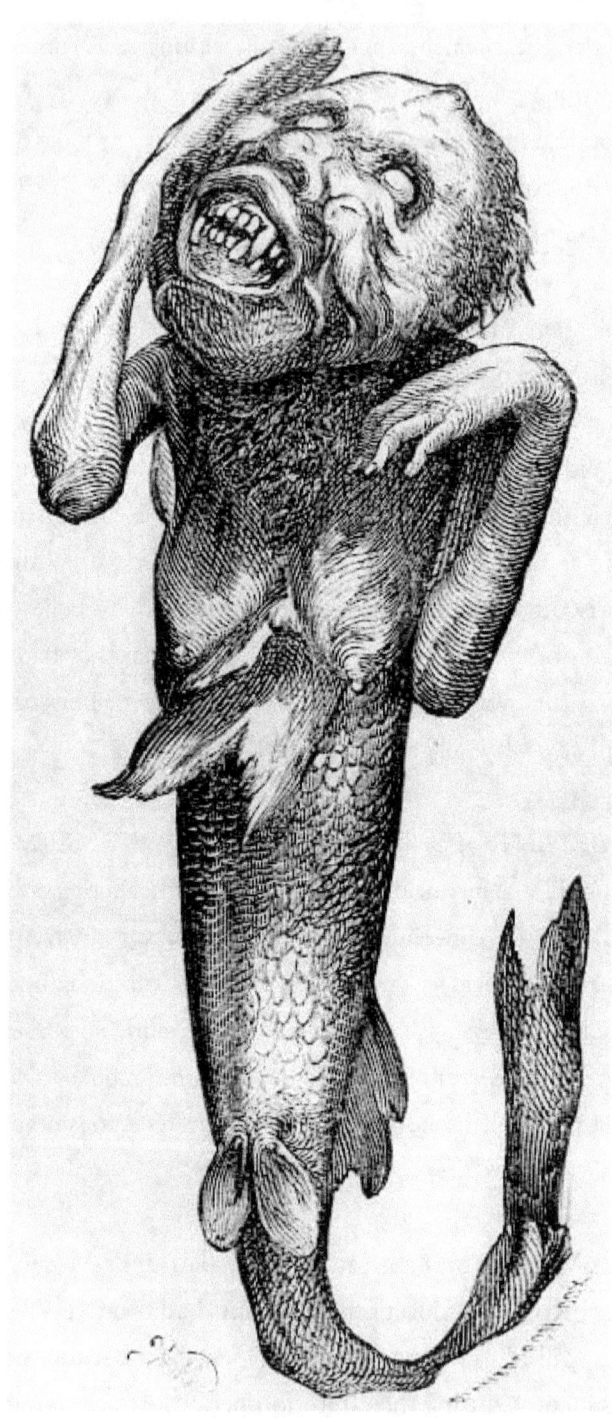

The Feeje Mermaid (Public domain image)

American Museum, the mermaid was taken around the country before being returned to Kimball in Boston.

In November 1842, Barnum was in Albany on business. Here he heard of an exceptionally small five-year-old child named Charles Stratton living in Bridgeport. Arranging to meet the child, Barnum found that he was 'the smallest child I have ever seen who could walk alone'. He was a dwarf and Barnum decided to engage him for his museum for four weeks at three dollars per week. The cost of all travel, board and lodging for Stratton and his mother were also to be borne by Barnum. At the end of the four weeks, Stratton was re-engaged by Barnum for a full year at seven dollars per week, with a bonus of 50 dollars at the end of the year. However, before the year was complete, Barnum had increased Stratton's payment to 25 dollars per week. Included in the terms of engagement was that both Stratton's parents would accompany him at Barnum's expense.

When he and his mother arrived in New York, Stratton was billed as 'General Tom Thumb, a dwarf of eleven years of age, just arrived from England!' There were three deceptions in this one sentence. Barnum had upped Stratton's age to make it clearer that he was a dwarf; he claimed that he was from England, thereby tapping into the concept of the 'exotic'; and he had given him the name of Tom Thumb. Tom Thumb was a well-known character in English folklore and *The History of Tom Thumb* was the first fairy tale published in English in 1621. The only surviving copy is said to be held by the Morgan Library and Museum of New York, along with several other seventeenth- and eighteenth-century manuscripts of the story. The character of Tom Thumb was well embedded in folklore even before this printing. There are certainly mentions of his name during the sixteenth century. In *The Discoverie of*

Witchcraft[6], Tom Thumb is one of several mentioned entities used to frighten children. In the story he is no larger than his father's thumb and he undergoes many adventures, including being swallowed by a cow, a fish, a giant, and a miller in various versions of the story. There are also references to Tom Thumb being in puddings[7], a popular image and something that happened regularly to 'kept' dwarfs throughout history.[8] The character Tom Thumb appeared on stage in Henry Fielding's *Tom Thumb* and in later works by William Hatchett and Eliza Haywood and also in stories such as *Hop o'My Thumb* and *Le Petit Poucet*.

The character of Tom Thumb would have been well known in America from colonial times and would have been embedded in children's stories by the time that Barnum came across Stratton. Renaming him as Tom Thumb tapped into this common image and drew upon the purported 'Englishness' of the character. Reinforcing this by giving him the title General raised the social status of an exotic character rooted in history and folklore. Barnum knew what he was doing.

The lives of Barnum and Stratton were to become inseparable over the next few years. Barnum was already an established figure within America and General Tom Thumb became the passport to international fame. At the end of 1842, at the age of 33, Barnum made the decision to take Stratton to Britain and Europe and introduce General Tom Thumb to the 'old country'.

Charles Stratton c.1845 (Library of Congress)

Notes

1   Woodward, W. (2012) *The War Connecticut Hated*. In Connecticut Explored Vol.10/No. 3 Summer 2012. Online at https://Connecticuthistory.org/the-war-connecticut-hated/

2   *The Herald of Freedom* 12 December 1832. Connecticut Digital Archive. Online at https://collections.ctdigitalarchive.org/islandora/object/60002%3A62#page/2/mode/2up

3   Barnum, P. T. (1869) *Struggles and Triumphs; Or, Forty Years' Recollections of P. T. Barnum*. Reprint 1981. Penguin Publishing Group.

4   *The Life of Joice Heth*. 1835 pamphlet. Documenting the American South. Online at https;//docsouth.unc.edu/neh/heth/heth.html

5   Reiss, B. (1999) *P. T. Barnum, Joice Heth and Antebellum Spectacles of Race*. American Quarterly, Vol. 51, No. 1 (March 1999) John Hopkins University Press.

6   Scot R. (1584) Reprint 1972. *The Discoverie of Witchcraft*. Dover Publications Inc. New York.

7   In *Coryat's Crudities* (1611) by James Field 'Tom Thumbe is dumbe, until the pudding creepe, in which he was intomb'd, then out doth peepe'. There is also a reference in Ben Johnson's masque *The Fortunate Isles*; 'Thomas Thumb in a pudding fat.'

8   In 1626, at a banquet given for King Charles 1 and his teenage wife Henrietta, the seven-year-old dwarf Jeffrey Hudson was presented to her in a pie. Similarly, during the 1760s, the dwarf Josef Boruwlaski, was presented in an urn at a banquet given by his 'owner' Countess Humiecka.

CHAPTER 2 – FAIRS, FREAKS AND HUMAN CURIOSITIES

When Barnum set sail for England, he was setting off for a country that was undergoing a prolonged period of social and political change. Britain had been committed to wars against the French for an almost unbroken period from 1793 to 1815, with an uneasy peace from 1801 to 1803. The so-called Napoleonic wars had seen Britain fighting campaigns in America, the Caribbean, South East Asia, Spain, Portugal, and France. Much of this was funded through the newly found wealth created by a growing industrial revolution, where Britain became the manufacturing powerhouse of the world. The country was changing from an agricultural to an industrial, capitalist, based economy. New mills and factories, especially in the north of England, were churning out products to be exported around the world by Britain's dominant seagoing trade.

With the defeat of Napoleon in 1815 at the Battle of Waterloo, one might have expected Britain to return to a time of peace and prosperity. But all was not well in the country. Many men returned from the wars broken and maimed. Unable to work, many relied on begging in the streets or applying to the poor houses to survive. Rural crafts and cottage industries were being overtaken by growing industrialisation and this, coupled with a gradual population shift from countryside to towns, created an agricultural depression. During the early nineteenth century the population also began to grow, and the labour supply was to become greater than the demand. Social unrest was the result.

Hand-loom weavers were hit particularly hard. A worker named Nedd Ludd gathered many followers who became known as 'General Ludd's Army' or, simply, 'Luddites'. Ludd led his groups in smashing up factory machines in the Midlands and Lancashire. Though the government responded by making machine-breaking a capital crime, the practice continued throughout the economic crisis. At the end of the war in 1815 it was expected by many that the price of food stuffs, particularly bread, would become lower. However, wealthy landowners complained that their income would collapse if this happened. Accordingly, the government introduced the Corn Law, which prohibited the import of cheap corn (in fact, all cereal grains such as wheat, barley, and oats) into Britain only when domestic prices hit 80 shillings a quarter [of a ton]. The ceiling price of 80 shillings was so high that it was never reached until 1845. This resulted in farmers' profits and the cost of bread remaining high. Poverty was rampant and unrest continued. The Corn Law would not be repealed until 1846.

Self-made wealthy industrialists demanded representation in parliament, which was dominated by the aristocracy who already had inherited wealth. Universal suffrage became the cry and was taken up by the working classes. In August 1819 a crowd of up to 60,000 working class people marched to St Peter's Field in Manchester to hear the Radical Reformer, Henry Hunt, give a speech. The Local magistrates, concerned that the meeting might result in a riot, had arranged for several hundred infantry and cavalry to be on standby on the day. Unnerved by the vast crowd that had gathered, and fearing insurrection, the magistrates ordered the waiting Manchester and Salford Yeomanry to arrest Henry Hunt as he arrived and before he could speak. It was questioned afterwards by the press as to whether the magistrates had expected trouble or had even manipulated the situation to ensnare Hunt:

The authorities seemed, indeed, to have had a presentiment of disturbance. They had ordered the ground to be cleared of stones and bricks some days previous to the meeting, that there might be no missiles with which to assail the military ... If there were warrants against Hunt previous to Monday [the day of the meeting], why was he not told of it on Saturday, when he offered to surrender himself? And if he was apprehended on account of remaining on the ground after the Riot Act was read, why was he not told that it was read before he entered the field? Was this a trap laid for convicting him of high treason? (*The Times* 20 August 1819)

Surrounded by angry protestors, the yeomanry panicked and the magistrates then sent in the 15th Hussars to clear the crowd. With sabres drawn they slashed their way through the throng. The crowd dispersed quickly, but not before 11 people were killed and 421 seriously wounded, many by sabre cuts to the head and upper torso. Disturbingly, over 100 victims were women and young children. The article in *The Times* gives us these details.

If the conduct of the magistrates was precipitate, that of the cavalry was violent and unwarrantable. It is allowed by everyone here that much unnecessary cruelty was inflicted ... They cut down and trampled under their horses' hoofs the poor deluded creatures who had assembled, without provocation and without mercy. I could send you the deposition of hundreds, if it were necessary, that not a stone was thrown, not a stick was raised, and not an insult offered to the military, before they commenced their furious career – that they trampled on those they could not disperse – that they hunted them down like wild beasts, and cut at the living heaps that were piled on each other in running from their violence.

Reports of the incident were published widely throughout Britain and the public was enraged at the callous way that the magistrates had dealt with the situation. Here was a Tory government in fear of revolution. It justified its actions by claiming that the gathering in St Peters' Field was one of sedition. Far from responding to the public outcry for reform, the Home Secretary Lord Sidmouth passed counter revolutionary Six Acts in late 1819. These limited the radical free press and constrained public meetings to being indoors and no more than 50 people from one parish. It also gave powers of stop and search to the yeomanry should they suspect anyone of harbouring weapons. It was not until a change of government that the Whigs brought about the 'Great' Reform Act of 1832 that widened the suffrage of men in Britain. Although only one in five men could actually vote, it did open the door for later reforms.

The Peterloo Massacre 1819 (Library of Congress)

It was against this backdrop of social and political upheaval that many of the old showmen found it hard going to maintain their exhibitions. The old fairs that were frequented by all were beginning to lose the middle-class patronage and were gradually closed down over a period of time. Governmental concerns over the fairs being a place where the working classes could gather added to this. As early as 1762 the Southwark Fair was closed, shortly followed by the May Fair in 1764. The trend continued into the nineteenth century, with Peckham Fair ceasing in 1827 and then Bartholomew Fair in 1855. Other fairs continued to close through 1860. Showmen were classed as 'rogues and vagabonds' and the law dealt severely with them (Sanger 1935:41). Subsequent legislation such as the Vagrancy Act of 1824, the Regulation of Markets and Fairs Act of 1847, and the Theatres Act of 1843 all added to the demise of the fairs in their old format.

George Sanger, later to become a renowned circus owner, grew up in a showman's family. Fairs at that time were unceremoniously rowdy. Charles Dickens captures the scene vividly;

> Imagine yourself in an extremely dense crowd, which swings you to and fro, and in and out, and every way but the right one; add to this the screams of women, the shouts of boys, the clanging of gongs, the firing of pistols, the ringing of bells, the bellowings of speaking-trumpets, the squeaking of penny dittos, the noise of a dozen bands, with three drums in each, all playing different tunes at the same time, the halloing of showmen, and the occasional roar from the wild beast shows; and you are in the very centre and heart of the fair (Dickens 1839)

Exhibitions of freaks were the mainstay of the fairs, although many of these turned out to be 'spoofs' created by unscrupulous (or perhaps creative?) showmen. Although the word 'humbug' was used in the English language as early as the mid-eighteenth century, it was not until the mid nineteenth century that it came into popular use to mean a 'fraud' or 'impostor'. The 1935 edition of Sanger's 1910 autobiography, recording his life as a nineteenth century travelling showman, makes the following observation;

> Perhaps the greatest change that has taken place in show-life in our generation is the disappearance of freaks and monstrosities; and this, it will surely be agreed by all, is a change entirely for the good. Of old, freaks were the mainstay of every show ... Yet freaks may still linger on, here and there (Sanger 1935:16-17)

Freaks, monstrosities, and human curiosities did still continue well into the nineteenth century but the nature of the 'freak show' was changing. The crude exhibition of such people for pure profit was now dressed up in a new respectability of ethnography and scientific enquiry; an educative activity. The scientific fields of Ethnography and Anthropology began to develop in the nineteenth century, both in the USA and in Europe. Scientists working in these newly-minted fields used two main modes of operation: study 'in the field' or having subjects brought to them for observation and examination. As the British Empire expanded, it was much easier to have 'human collections' brought to England. Thus, we witness the rise of 'human zoos', a family group, individual, or a tribal group displayed for scientific study and popular entertainment. Ethnographic scenes were created and were promoted as to amuse, inform, and educate. When a Japanese Village was created in London in 1885 the *London and China Express* reported that,

An exhibition of a distinctly novel character will shortly be opened at Kensington, which, from an ethnographical point of view, will doubtless interest the public. The show will consist of a Japanese village, which is being erected in Humphreys Hall and on the surrounding ground ... There will altogether be about 200 Japanese men, women, and children in the village (*London and China Express* 5 December 1884)

It is interesting that the event is described as both an exhibition and a show, incorporating both the idea of the scientific and the entertaining. During the 'show', ladies could have their hair dressed in the Japanese fashion and a photographic booth was available for people to be photographed in Japanese clothing. Shops and a restaurant were also on site.

Some of these 'shows' could be displayed in many venues; the science laboratory, a zoological park, an exhibition hall, at a world fair, in the music hall, or even at a circus.

... a visit to the zoological gardens, to the circus or to a 'negro village', was not just a chance to witness the diversity of humanity, it was an opportunity for the visitor to understand not only the Other's place in the world, but also his own (Barthe & Coutancier, 1995 cited Blanchard et al 2008:24)

Human zoos said little about the subjects on exhibition. They were little more than a display of how the white Europeans thought 'inferior' races should be portrayed. These questionable exhibitions fed the public's need to clarify its own identity; the Self vs the Other. Growing imperial expansion established two broad racial worlds; the world of the ruling colonisers and the world of the subjugated natives. Commercial exploitation of these exotic groups was rife.

Perhaps the most infamous case in nineteenth century Britain was that of the 'Hottentot Venus'. Sawtche (Sara) Bartmann was born in the East Cape area of modern South Africa. She was enslaved as a child and then bought by a Dutch naval doctor who brought her to England in 1810. She was humiliatingly exhibited throughout the country in a tight-fitting costume so as to appear naked and men and women of all persuasions paid money to gape at her and even to touch her. A popular ballad of the time reflects just how much of an attraction she became (Frith 2005);

> Well go no more to other shows while Venus treads the stage
> We'll go no more to other shows while Hottentot's the rage

Being exotic was equated with being sexually appealing. She was displayed with little more sensitivity than a wild animal. A report in *The Times* stated that;

> The deponent had gone to the exhibition; that he there found a stage raised about three feet from the floor, with a cage, or enclosed place at the end of it; that the Hottentot was within the cage; that on being ordered by her keeper, she came out, and that her appearance was highly offensive to delicacy ... The Hottentot was produced like a wild beast, and ordered to move backwards and forwards, and come out and go into her cage, more like a bear in a chain than a human being ... She frequently heaved deep sighs; seemed anxious

Sara Bartmann. Early 19th century caricature (Westminster archives)

and uneasy; grew sullen, when she was ordered to play on some rude instrument of music (*The Times* 26 November 1810)

Many, scientists apart, visited the exhibition out of curiosity and the appearance of Bartmann aroused mixed emotions. It has to be remembered that in the early 19th century in Britain there was a strong abolitionist movement against enslavement.

I knew not that such a being was in existence until passing by the house of exhibition in Piccadilly, near the Haymarket, the advertisements in the window caught my eye; and ignorant of what sight I was to see, - a sight disgraceful both to decency and humanity, - I entered. A small stage was erected in the room, and some slight scenes, representing an African hut, &c. were placed around it; from this hut the poor unhappy woman came forth, like a dog, at the call of its master. Never in my life did I feel my pity more strongly excited; with no other clothing than a tight dress, the colour of her skin, and a few rude ornaments, such as are worn by the nations of South Africa, the dreadful deformity of her person was fully displayed; and her face, spite of the paint, with which, after the manner of her country, it was daubed, was strongly and deeply marked with misery. I mentioned this to her master, but he said that 'she was sick and sulky, and was always sulky when company was there' (*The Examiner* 14 October 1810)

Her 'dreadful deformity' was a particular physical anatomy, steatopygia and macronymphy, and these were the subject of scientific debate. It was clear to doctors and scientists that she was an example of the black race's inferiority. She died in Paris in 1815, at the early age of 26. Her humiliation continued after her death, as she was dissected and her skeleton and body cast were displayed for many years in the Musée de l'Homme, until 1975. It was only in 2002 that her remains were returned to South Africa and interred near the place of her birth.

The case of Sara Bartmann was very much still in the vein of the exhibition of human curiosities that were seen at travelling fairs but now it was becoming more of a commercial enterprise in a private exhibition space. As fairs gradually began to close there was an underlying intention for such exhibitions to appeal more to the middle classes. This attitude was clearly displayed with the arrival in London of conjoined twins, known as Chang and Eng, from America in November 1829. The twins were reputedly born in 1811 in Siam (now Thailand), although they may have been ethnically Chinese. Although joined by a band of connective tissue at the chest, they lived a peaceful and happy life. It was in 1820 when a British merchant encountered the boys. Seeing the potential for profit making, he and his partner Abel Coffin struck a deal with the boys' mother and entered into negotiations with the king of Siam to 'buy' the boys. The king finally agreed after several years and the twins were first taken to America. On arrival in England, Coffin set them up in the rooms of the Egyptian Hall for public exhibition. As well as being displayed as human curiosities, the twins later developed an 'act' that included leaping and somersaults. In this way, the twins moved beyond the ethnographic and scientific exhibition to the realm of the 'freak show'. Preceding the opening to the public, a private viewing was held for eminent scientists and the press. The *English Chronicle and Whitehall Evening Post* of the 26th of November was at pains to stress the acceptability of such an exhibition.

We were yesterday admitted to a private inspection, at the Egyptian Hall, of the two Siamese youths, whose bodies are, in a manner so unexampled, inseparably attached to each other. The exhibition of monstrous formations in general is liable to great objection. In this country such sights, for good reasons, are also obnoxious to suspicion. We say this in order at once, and most unequivocally, to separate the phenomenon of which we now speak from almost every other exhibition of human malformation, real or pretended, that has ever engaged the attention of the public. Indeed, to our apprehension the curiosity on this occasion is not so much a physical as it is of a moral character; and in the latter point of view these boys become, in our judgement, a deeply impressive and even affecting sight. It is proper therefore to dismiss at once the objection that this spectacle is either disgusting or even displeasing; on the contrary, we speak only the opinions of the most eminent professional men of the day when we assert that there is nothing in the whole course of the exhibition which can be deemed repugnant to the bashfulness of the most fastidious of the gentler sex ... We repeat that there is nothing in the exhibition which the most timid maiden may not endure – whilst the most hardened cannot fail to be struck with the manifestations which they give of generous, kindly, and affectionate natures.

As well as underlining the acceptability of the exhibition, the above article also goes into a lengthy pseudo-scientific appraisal of the boys' behaviour as twins, with comments from some of the notable scientists of the day present. With Queen Adelaide and other members of the aristocracy visiting the exhibition, this also reinforced the respectability

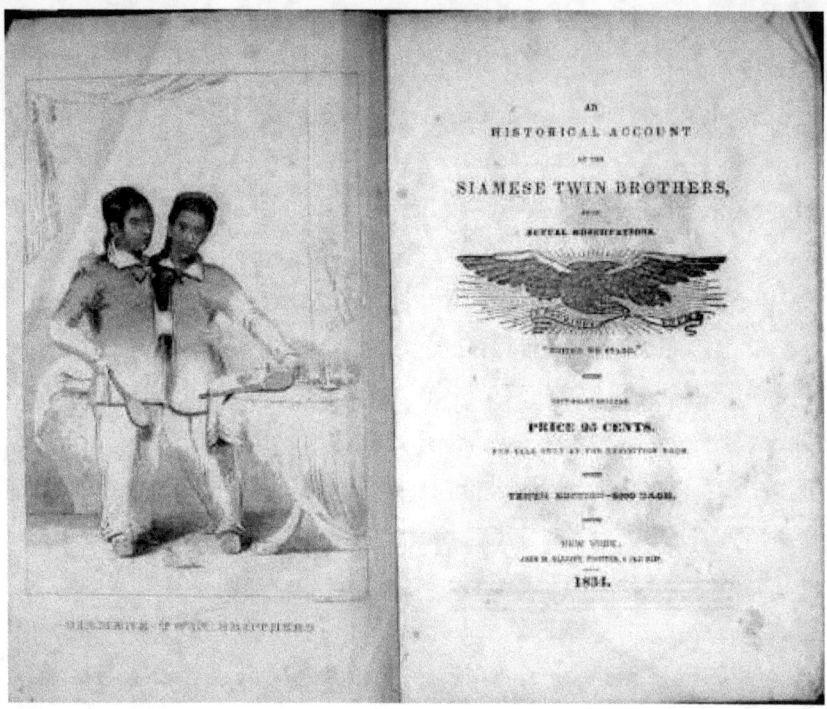

Siamese Twin Brothers. 1834 pamphlet for the exhibition of Chang and Eng (American Social History Project)

of the exhibition. A report from the previous day gives a description of the youths.

> Their attire was made to resemble, as nearly as possible, the costume of their native country. The front part of their heads was closely cropped, and over the back part of the crown the hair, which is there suffered to grow at great length, was wound into a graceful, platted wreath. The persons of these boys exactly resemble the figures of the Chinese, which may be frequently seen in the shops in London (*London Packet and New Lloyd's Evening Post* 25 November 1829)

In 1830, the twins were toured throughout Britain, reaching as far north as Scotland. The twins were then taken to France, where they were not so well received, before returning to America.

There were times in their lives when it was suggested that an attempt should be made to separate them. The twins themselves were never very keen on this idea. There was also a reluctance on the part of physicians, as medical science had not advanced enough to make the procedure safe for both youths. Sir Astley Cooper, an eminent surgeon and anatomist, when asked if he would consider separating them said that he would not like to try and why separate them when the two boys seemed quite happy as they were. He also made the point to Coffin that the two would make much more money while they were together than if they were separated.[1] This raises the question of exploitation and to what extent Chang and Eng were in control of their own destinies. I think that there was a genuine scientific interest from the medical fraternity in their condition. But for the average person, the twins were an 'exotic other'; they were from a different culture, thereby feeding into ethnographic curiosity but they were also human curiosities, thus allowing a voyeuristic public to be simultaneously fascinated and repulsed. Certainly, a lot of money was made for Coffin in their names. Entrance to the exhibitions was a flat rate 1 shilling and 'Historic booklets, with full length portrait'[2] were sold at 6d per copy. It was reported that 100,000 people visited the exhibition in London and a further 200,000 saw the exhibition as it travelled throughout the provinces. 2,000 copies of the booklet were also sold. That generated a gross income in excess of £15,000 (more than £1 million in today's money). In 1832 the twins broke away from Coffin and toured under their own auspices, before settling down in Surry County, N C, in 1839.. They briefly returned to touring in the early 1850s and then were engaged by Barnum in 1860 to exhibit at his

American Museum. However, they did not get on with Barnum and rejected his offer of an extended engagement.

Were they happy being exhibited? Although they seemed to have had a better experience than Sara Bartmann, they were still treated as objects to be exhibited for profit. There are some who would argue that had the twins been left in their village they would probably have eked out a living as fishermen and lived a contented life doing so. Being exhibited by Coffin did broaden their experience and allow them some form of income, however meagre. This argument does not question the moral issue of individuals being 'enslaved' for the profit of others—no matter how that enslavement is dressed up. Unlike Sara Bartmaan, the exploitation of Chang and Eng was never legally challenged. In 1810 her case was brought before the Attorney-General by the African Society, an Abolitionist organisation, seeking a writ of Habeus Corpus to ensure that Bartmann was taken into care and then, ultimately, to be returned to her homeland. The Attorney-General ruled against this and subsequent challenges to this ruling were made. The appeal case was made in November 1810 on the two grounds that the exhibition was *contra bonos mores* (against good morals), and that Bartmann was kept under improper restraint. Arguments were made on both sides, very much hinging on whether she had willingly entered into engagement with her manager to be taken from South Africa for exhibition. Lord Ellenborough, the Lord Chief Justice, gave the following summing up to the appeal case;

> If the exhibition in question, should be conducted in such a manner as to occasion an indecent exposure of the person, so as to violate the laws of morality, there was a mode of bringing the exhibitors to punishment, and of preventing the continuance of

the exhibition. That was not a case, however, to which the Court were now called on to direct their consideration. If there had been any unlawful restraint too, exercised on the inclinations of the person exhibited, that also would have been a good ground for the interference of the Court. Here, however, there was no pretence for any idea of the kind. The party, supposed to be under restraint, had, in express terms, declared the reverse. She had no desire of changing her present situation, or of returning to her native country. The application therefore fell to the ground. Rule discharged (*Pilot (London)* 29 November 1810)

Chang and Eng never had the luxury of expressing their views in a public court. They were, however, discontented with some aspects of how they were treated. On removal from their homeland, they had been brought to Britain as steerage passengers, whilst their 'owner', Abel Coffin and his party, travelled in first class luxury. Coffin had a very paternalistic attitude towards them. Indeed, in one of the exhibition pamphlets it was written that; 'For Captain Coffin and his Lady, they have a paternal regard, calling them very frequently father and mother' (Woolf 2019:118). This is something that most human exhibits seemed to have experienced; to be treated in a child-like manner, thereby reinforcing the concept of white imperial power. It is something that will be seen again in Barnum's relationship with Tom Thumb. By January 1831, they had returned to America under the direct management of Coffin's domineering wife Susan; Coffin was travelling further in the Far East. Under her management they embarked on a gruelling and relentless tour of America. Whereas in Britain they were able to be exhibited in halls and theatre and other more 'respectable' venues, on the American tour they were little more than itinerant entertainers being presented in railway houses and mud shows. The twins resented this so much that in May 1832 they cancelled their contract with the Coffins and became 'their own men'. Although they continued to tour, they were now exhibitors rather than exhibits. This was important because they could choose when and where they exhibited and, more importantly, they could keep the profits for themselves. They were now independent self-employed entertainers. When they did eventually retire from the business in 1839, they had amassed a significant amount of money that enabled them to purchase a 1,000-acre farm. By the early 1840s they had settled down in North Carolina and went on to marry sisters Adelaide and Sarah Yates. Between them, they produced 21 offspring. They died

Chang and Eng in later life c.1870 (Public domain image)

within hours of each other in 1874, still bound together by that band of connective tissue.

Bartmann and the Siamese twins marked a transitionary stage in the history of the freak show in Britain. The old itinerant fairground booths of the days of George Sanger were in decline and the freak show was beginning to take on a semblance of 'respectability', with exhibitions taking place in private rooms or in large public halls in major towns and cities. This contrasts with the ongoing nature of the travelling freak show that perpetuated in America for many decades, even if Barnum was beginning to exhibit in a permanent venue. Human curiosities, the 'freaks', were still regularly displayed in travelling shows. Although set in the depression era of the 1930s, a short film entitled *The Butterfly Circus*[3] gives an example of how such a travelling show must have appeared, both from the point of view of the audience and those being exhibited. The travelling sideshow portrayed and the exhibition at the Egyptian Hall in London seem very different. For Barnum, Britain was an unknown world and one that he was about to set foot in.

Notes

1   *English Chronicle and Whitehall Evening Post* 26 November 1829.

2   *Leeds Patriot and Yorkshire Advertiser* 23 October 1830.

3   *The Butterfly Circus* (2009) Online at Bing Videos.

CHAPTER 3 – AN UNKNOWN LAND

The First Class Packet Ship – The Yorkshire (Public domain image)

Barnum, aged 33 years, five feet ten and a quarter inch tall, with a medium forehead, dark eyes, prominent nose, small mouth, round chin, brown hair, a light and florid complexion, and an oval face,[1] arrived on board *The Yorkshire* in Liverpool England on the 7th of February 1844. He left his wife Charity and their three daughters, Caroline, Helen, and Frances at home in America, although the third daughter Frances would tragically die only two months after his arrival in England. Contrary to popular imagery as portrayed in the most recent film about the man, *The Greatest Showman*, he did not travel with a full entourage of performers. In his autobiography he would have us believe that;

A large throng of persons were gathered upon the wharves, and many were anxiously inquiring for Tom Thumb, as it had previously been announced in Liverpool that he would arrive in the Yorkshire [Packet Ship]. His mother managed to smuggle him on shore without being noticed, for they little thought that he was small enough to be carried in arms, like an infant. (Barnum 1855)

The British press was strangely silent on this matter and no mention is made of a 'reception' by a thriving throng. The *Liverpool Albion* of 12 February 1844 merely gives us a list of passengers;

THE PACKET-SHIP YORKSHIRE. This splendid ship, commanded by Captain Bailey, arrived at this port on Wednesday morning last. She made Holyhead in eighteen and a half days, having left New York on the 18th ultimo. She brought fourteen passengers, a list of whom we subjoin; Gen. Tom Thumb and servant, P.T. Barnum Esq., S.E. Stratton and lady, J.W. Holberton, Edmund G. Simpson, Thomas W. Braidwood, E. Gilliam, George Cisco, New York; Robert Waller, Philadelphia; James Dick, W. T. Whitehead, William Roy, Montreal; Louis Mark Esq., bearer of despatches.

In fact, more column inches were given over to a passenger's report on the conditions of the voyage, which apparently was unseasonably warm and passage delayed because of slight winds for at least five days.

Given the tumultuous send-off that Barnum's party had received on leaving America, as here recorded in the *New York Times*;

Not less than ten thousand persons joined in procession yesterday, to escort this wonderful little man on board the ship Yorkshire, by which splendid packet he has sailed, in company with his parents and Mr. Barnum, proprietor of the American Museum, for the purpose of visiting Her Majesty Queen Victoria and the nobility of England. The procession passed down Fulton-street, preceded by the city brass band. The General was in an open barouche, and bowed very gracefully to the thousands of ladies who filled the windows on each side of the street, and who testified their delight at seeing him by the waving of thousands of white handkerchiefs. The shipping adjacent to the Yorkshire was black with the multitude gathered to witness the departure of the smallest man and finest ship that the world ever produced. Our little countryman will astonish the citizens of the old world ...

It is a little surprising that Barnum's advance publicity did not generate more coverage of his, and especially that of General Tom Thumb's, arrival. There had been advanced press about Tom Thumb during 1843—as early as August—but in this instance, it was only a copy of an advertisement for the American Museum;

GEN. TOM THUMB Jun. The smallest person that ever walked alone! Can be seen during the whole day and evening. He will be DRESSED AS A YANKEE SAILOR! And at each performance he will sing a Patriotic Song. He is 11 years old and WEIGHS ONLY FIFTEEN POUNDS! (*Illustrated London Life* 13 August 1843)

Other mentions of his name merely gave facts;

EXTRAORDINARY DWARF. The 'New York Journal of Medicine' gives an account of a boy, named Charles Stratton, six or seven years of age, who weighed at birth nine pounds two ounces, but who now is but twenty-two inches tall (*Hereford Journal* 25 October 1843)

The following item also appeared in the *Perthshire Courier* on 2 November 1843, but it wasn't until the December that a full description of Tom Thumb's attributes is given;

We may shortly expect from America one of the rarest curiosities in human shape nature has yet produced ... 'General Tom Thumb' ... The 'General' as he is familiarly called, will be twelve years of age on the 11th of January next, and now stands exactly twenty-five inches high, and weighs fifteen pounds one ounce. Notwithstanding his extreme minuteness he is beautifully proportioned in every part, and his face is intelligent and open. He has a florid complexion, light hair, beautiful well-opened dark eyes, and a forehead ample for his size. In air and manner he is already manly, and polite and vivacious in his demeanour. He is well informed, extremely quick, and all the force of nature which should have been fairly bestowed on the growth of his body seems to have been spent in the expansion of his intellectual faculties. He is always dressed in the height of fashion, and, as he comports himself with the easy grace of an exquisite, the contrast between his appearance and that of other people is the more surprising. His head scarcely reaches so high as the seat of a chair, and an ordinary table affords him a very pretty promenade. The cane he carries in his hand resembles a steel pen holder, and his glossy beaver hat is about the size of a teacup. His hands and feet, from having been little used, are exquisitely delicate in their proportions, and appear to great advantage, the former in Lilliputian yellow kid gloves, and the latter in Wellingtons of the finest Spanish leather. It is stated that at his birth nothing extraordinary was noticed in his appearance, but that when he was about six months old it was remarked he did not grow. Curiosity prompted his parents to weigh him at that time, and he was found to be exactly the weight he is now, fifteen pounds. He has never varied above an ounce or two in the interval, and has never increased in stature one hair's breadth. His appetite is excellent. He picks the bones of a lark or the merrythought of a partridge with keen relish, and tosses off his wine (his glass is as large as a thimble) with the air of a *bon vivant*. He is a great admirer of female society, and boasts of having rifled the sweets, in one of his southern tours, of 6,000 pairs of the fairest ladies' lips in America ... He sails from New York for England on the 1st of January and is full of triumph at the idea of his anticipated conquests. Sam Slick's description of the beauty of English women has thrown him into ecstasies, and quite reconciled him to the perils of the voyage (*Cambridge Chronicle and Journal* 30 December 1843)

Certainly, this is enough information to pique the interest of the British public but it only appeared in a provincial newspaper, and one that was the opposite side of the country to Liverpool. It is hardly likely that people would make the several-hundred-mile journey from Cambridgeshire to Liverpool to witness the arrival of an American dwarf. In fact, in all the pre-notifications of his arrival no date or time is given and there is no record of any notification at all in the local Liverpool press. So, did Barnum have a local agent 'on the ground' in Liverpool who was responsible for releasing pre-arrival flyers and posters or is the 'large throng' he refers to another of his exaggerations? As far as I am aware, there are no extant flyers or posters from this event.

Another interesting point is that Barnum makes the comment that Tom Thumb was smuggled ashore in his mother's arms, as an infant. It begs the question as to why? For a man who believed in publicity and promotion, I find it strange that he would not have taken this opportunity to be in the public eye and to gain press coverage. For Barnum, Britain was uncharted territory. For all his ballyhoo about travelling to the 'old country' to visit Queen Victoria and the nobility, he may have been unsure about exactly how the British public would react to Tom Thumb. As we have seen earlier in the previous chapter, British attitudes towards 'freaks' were markedly different from America and I am sure that Barnum would have wanted to present his charge to the British public on his own terms. There was also the matter that America and Britain had been at war only 32 years previously[2] and maybe he was also unsure of how Americans might be received in Britain. Another possibility was, of course, that Barnum was holding back from revealing Tom Thumb so soon, thereby raising the anticipation of the British public. We should remember at this point that any exhibition or presentation of "Tom Thumb" was a performance by Charles Stratton, under the direction of Barnum. Stratton was not Tom Thumb but only took on that persona when exhibiting to the public. Therefore, it was to better advantage for Barnum's purposes that Tom Thumb was presented in a controlled environment, such as a theatre.

Unable to travel immediately to London and achieve his stated ambition of being presented to the Queen, the royal court being in mourning over the death of Prince Albert's father, Barnum secured the use of a public hall in Liverpool to premiere Tom Thumb to the public. Within a week of landing in Britain, Tom Thumb made his first appearance on British soil in the Portico;

TOM THUMB ARRIVED!

CHARLES S. STRATTON, known as GENERAL TOM THUMB Jnr.

THE AMERICAN DWARF! Is happy to announce to the Ladies and Gentlemen of Liverpool, that he has arrived, in good health and spirits, from his native land, and will have the honour of making his appearance before the British Public THIS DAY, the 12th instant, at the PORTICO, NEWINGTON, BOLD-STREET, where he may be seen for a few days only.

GENERAL TOM THUMB Jun. is twelve years old, TWENTY-FIVE INCHES HIGH, and WEIGHS ONLY FIFTEEN POUNDS!! That having been his precise weight when only six months old. He is of fine symmetrical proportions, very graceful, and manly in his manners; lively, sociable, and intelligent. He will amuse his Visitors with a variety of Songs, Dances, &c.

TOM THUMB Jun. was visited in America by more than Half a Million of Ladies and Gentlemen, of the highest distinction, who universally pronounced him the SMALLEST PERSON WHO EVER WALKED ALONE!

Hours of Exhibition from Ten, a.m., to Four, p.m., and in the Evening from Six to Nine. (*Liverpool Albion* 12 February 1844)

The above advertisement, possibly penned by Barnum and certainly approved by him, raises some interesting observations. Firstly, Tom Thumb is labelled as 'Jnr.' This might imply that there was a Tom Thumb Snr., although there is no record of this. Secondly, Tom Thumb is 'on stage' for a total of eight hours during any day at the Portico. When the average length of a play in a theatre is in the region of two hours, this is a tremendous amount of time for a supposed 12-year-old to perform. Stratton had certainly been well schooled by Barnum in his performance. And here lies the final point. Barnum portrays Stratton as being twelve years old but already the British press had reported that the *New York Journal of Medicine* had recorded his age as being six or seven years. However, in the official register of Passport Applications 1843 - 1846 (National Archives and Records Administration), Barnum has Charles Stratton listed as being 12 years old. This was one of Barnum's greatest deceptions, and one that he later did not deny. In his autobiography, Barnum recounts how he had discovered Charles S. Stratton in Bridgeport, Connecticut in 1842:

> He was only five years old, and to exhibit a dwarf of that age might provoke the question. How do you know that he is a dwarf? Some licence might indeed be taken with the facts, but even with this advantage I really felt that the adventure was nothing more than an experiment... They arrived in New York on Thanksgiving Day, Dec. 8, 1842, and Mrs Stratton was greatly astonished to find her son heralded in my Museum bills as Gen. TOM THUMB, a dwarf of eleven years of age, just arrived from England. This announcement contained two deceptions. I shall not attempt to justify them but may be allowed to plead the circumstances in extenuation. The boy was undoubtedly a dwarf, and I had the most reliable evidence that he had grown little, if any, since he was six months old; but

had I announced him as only five years of age, it would have been impossible to excite the interest or awaken the curiosity of the public. The thing I aimed at was, to assure them that he really was a dwarf – and in this, at least, they were not deceived … I took great pains to train my diminutive prodigy, devoting many hours to that purpose, by day and by night, and succeeded, because he had native talent and an intense love of the ludicrous. (Barnum 1855)

To what extent can Barnum be said to be guilty of exploiting this child for his own profit, even if Stratton and his parents did well out of the tour? Here was a child of around five years old who was engaged by Barnum to be exhibited in his museum. He was given the persona of General Tom Thumb and intensively schooled to present himself as at least six years older than he really was, and what is more, to present that fictitious 12-year-old as a young adult male. Did Barnum have an awareness of the sensitivity in Britain towards child exploitation, particularly in the workplace? It is possible and perhaps this also added to his caution on arrival in Britain. As Nardelli (1980:1) commented;

The industrial revolution had transformed Great Britain from a nation of agricultural villages into a nation of factory towns. Many of the social changes accompanying industrialisation aroused the indignation of contemporary critics.

Thompson (1963:349) goes on to write that;

The exploitation of little children, on this scale and with this intensity, was one of the most shameful events in our history.

The first Factory Act of 1833 banned children under the age of nine years old from being employed, specifically in factories. In theory this act was also to have been applied to all forms of child employment, including the theatre. It also limited children aged nine to 12 years to nine hours per day. Later Acts in 1844 and 1874 would improve on this and raise the age limits from eight to 12 to 10 to 13. The employment of children in the theatre (and in other occupations) was a contentious issue that was debated at length in parliament. Even as late as 1889, after the House of Lords had debated and suggested amendments to *The Prevention of Cruelty to and the Protection of Children Bill (no.372), 14 August 1889*[3], the matter was further debated in the House of Commons. Mr H. Fowler, Member of Parliament for Wolverhampton East stated;

> ... with reference to the licensing of children under 10 years of age for theatrical performances. The House [of Commons] will recollect that we carried by large majorities, both in Committee and on the Report, a provision that no child under 10 should, under any circumstances, be allowed to sing or play for profit, either in a theatre or in a circus. We applied the Factory Act to theatrical performances ... but the alteration that the House of Lords has made is this – although it leaves the clause precisely as it was with reference to children under seven years of age, as to children between 7 and 10, power is given to a Petty Sessional Court to grant licenses for such employment ... Now, I regret that amendment, but we have to deal with this matter as practical men ... I hope that the House will, as a matter of wise and judicious policy, agree with the Amendment, and thus permit the Bill, which will be a great boon to the children of this country, to become law without any further delay.

The amendments were agreed to and subsequently passed into law, but there were still those who, although they may have voted in favour of those amendments at that time, were setting out their stance to further lobby for a definitive age limit under which no child should be employed. In the same debate as given above, Mr Winterbotham, Member of Parliament for Cirencester, made the following point;

> With regards to this amendment, I may add that, though it is agreed to at present, it will not prevent the fight from being renewed and carried on until the labour of all children under ten years is, without exception, prohibited.

It was not until 1903 that the minimum age for child actors was finally set at 10 years old. By actively promoting Tom Thumb as being 11 or 12 years old, Barnum could argue, if challenged, that he was employing a child at the upper limit of the regulations for only eight hours per day. Stratton was under contract as Tom Thumb on a salary of US $50 per week plus living costs and transport during his visit to Britain and Europe and was therefore certainly employed by Barnum as his manager.

How did Barnum present Tom Thumb to the British public? There is no review of his appearance at the Portico in Liverpool and Barnum makes no reference to it in his autobiography. The above advertisement alludes to 'songs, dances &c.'—although exactly what the '&c.' was, is not given. By the 16th of February, Barnum had secured an exhibition of Stratton at the Royal Liver Theatre as an adjunct to a theatrical performance by Mr Phelps:

> Mr Phelps' Benefit – It will be seen, by the advertisement, that the benefit of this distinguished tragedian will take place at the Royal

Liver Theatre, this evening when he will appear as Othello. Tom Thumb, the American dwarf, makes his appearance in some of the Grecian statues (*Liverpool Mercury* 16 February 1844)

The Grecian statues were a series of tableaux, in which Stratton presented a variety of classical images. It would seem that his exhibition at the Royal Liver Theatre coincided with his appearance at the Portico, for in advertising for the Portico, Barnum is at pains to point out that;

His engagement at the Theatre-Royal, Church-street, (Late Liver Theatre) will in no manner interfere with his exhibition on the same night at the Portico (*Liverpool Mercury* 16 February 1844)

Barnum was certainly making Stratton work hard. Fortunately, Church Street and Bold Street are not too far apart, being on either side of Hanover Street. Although appearing in at least two venues in Liverpool, there is no record as to how Tom Thumb had been received. Fitzsimons (1969) maintains that the Liverpool exhibitions were poorly attended, although he gives no evidence for this. His rationale is that he considers that the ordinary people of Liverpool would not wish to pay the relatively excessive entrance fee of one shilling to see a dwarf. Dwarfs and other so termed 'freaks' were staple attractions at fairs and other places of low entertainment, where entrance fees of no more than one penny would be charged. Barnum wanted to present his dwarf in a much more refined image, especially as his intention was eventually to be presented to Queen Victoria. He gambled that, with the right promotion, people would be prepared to pay to see Tom Thumb, the American dwarf. The hoped for success of his Liverpool exhibitions would pave the way for his work in London.

P T Barnum and Tom Thumb c.1845 (National Portrait Gallery)

And so, on the 18th of February, Barnum moved his small company to the metropolis. He took a furnished suite of rooms in Grafton Street, Mayfair, a fashionable and fairly exclusive part of the city. Today, properties in that area can be priced in the region of £70 million. Barnum's neighbours were Lord Brougham and several other members of the British aristocracy. While still waiting for an opportunity to broach the ambition to visit Buckingham Palace, he had secured an engagement for Stratton for a short series of exhibitions at the Princess's Theatre. These exhibitions were to be given in the interval between acts two and three of the opera *Don Pasquale*. On Tuesday the 20th of February he made his début. *The Era* of the 25th of February gave a full and lengthy review;

> On Tuesday evening a 'great' *effect* was produced here by a very little *cause*; the rush into the house at half-price would have told the most incurious that something attractive was on the 'tapis' [stage], without reference to the bill itself, which bore in Brobdignag[4] letters the 'début' of the hero of Lilliput – the Pride of Kentucky – the Monarch of Dwarfs – General Tom Thumb! For our own part we armed ourselves with a 'lorgnette' of extra lens [a pair of spectacles on a handle], and determined not only to see the minute freak of nature, should it be a palpable embodiment of flesh and blood, but to see through it if it were not   the curtain had descended on '*Don Pasquale*'; the orchestra remained inactive; the audience was mute; the bell tinkles; the gorgeous drop-scene rises; and from the wings enters – a long, lank gentleman, agile enough seemingly for a hunter of indigenous Indians, and looking as hungry as a cannibal; this personage was Mr Barnum, the respected proprietor of the Museum at New York, who obligingly intimated that his little friend, the General, would, with the permission of those he saw

around him, make his first bow to the British public. No sooner said than done: far up the stage ... emerging through a door, a little dark spec is visible ... pitter-patter, an infant that has by some magic process, jumped out of its cradle, and abjured its pap for popularity, advances towards the stage-lights; can it speak as well as walk, aye, and sing too in notes both audible and laudable;

Yankee Doodle came to town....

Language positively fails in depicting the thrill of wonder, blent [blended] with admiration, that ran through the house ... The 'conductor' [Barnum] reaches down his paw to his '*confrére*', who is on the wrong side of his knee, when, holding in one hand a cane, the Hercules, as well as Apollo, grasping it with both, is lifted high in the air ... An imitation of Bonaparte, and really to the life, was next given, amidst thunders of applause ... and late in the evening, a string of personations were offered upon a table, of what are conventionally termed 'the Grecian Statues' – Mars, the Gladiator, Hercules, Ajax defying the Lightning, Sampson carrying the Gates of Gaza, the African alarmed at the Thunder, were successively embodied, but the most perfect *tableau* was Cupid with his wings and quiver, and the bow that does such mischief ... We almost omitted to mention that the 'General' danced a Hornpipe with such vigour and precision ... the sole drawback in seeing him consisted in the painful evidence that he was suffering under a severe cold. A screen had been subsequently placed at his back when performing the 'statues', which adds to the effect and shelters him from the draft. The hero of the evening was called before the curtain at the close of his performance, he bowed his acknowledgements in the most graceful and collected manner.

General Tom Thumb in his different characters. Small poster c.1850 (Barnum Museum, Bridgeport, Connecticut)

His appearance at the Princess's Theatre was covered by most of the London newspapers, and some provincial newspapers, although not all as kindly as in *The Era*. *The Globe* (21 February) commented that 'the little treble-pipe voice in which he spoke excited a good deal of laughter' and the *Shipping and Mercantile Gazette* of the same date wrote that 'on his first entrance he was greeted with shouts of laughter and surprise'. The *Illustrated London News* (24 February) opined that 'The production of this little monster affords another melancholy proof of the *low* state the legitimate drama has been reduced to!' and was also very sceptical about his actual age; 'He is stated, in a pamphlet printed in New York, to have been born Jan. 11, 1832; but of this we are somewhat sceptical'. *The Weekly Dispatch (London)* was more critical;

> His appearance was very ludicrous, and created a hearty laugh in the theatre; it was like Gulliver's arrival in Brobdignag ... This little fellow's voice is, from his small formation, very weak and shrill ... His performance of 'The Grecian Statues' on a table was not the least interesting portion of his exhibition. ... Whether this be a proper place for such performances, and whether it would not have been in more accordance with taste to display this little creature at a place devoted solely to the purposes of ocular gratification, may be a question (25 February)

Bell's Life in London was also critical of his appearance;

> In the subsequent part of the evening he attempted imitations of the Grecian and other statutes. In this part of the performance the General was not so happy as where he was more modernly attired, his head appearing somewhat too large in the tight dress; and,

indeed, this miniature edition of a man possesses a frontispiece which is slightly disproportioned to the volume (25 February)

The week at the Princess's Theatre was Barnum's first exhibition in the metropolis and it may not have been everything that he had hoped it would be. Was it a success? True, it had given public exposure to his prodigy, Tom Thumb, and the subsequent publicity it had engendered would have done him no harm. After all, all publicity can be good publicity if handled correctly. The newspaper reviews of the week's exhibition had been very mixed, The *Illustrated London News* of the 2nd of March perhaps summing up;

> The production of the diminutive prodigy 'Tom Thumb' has failed in general. We are not sorry for it, although we regret at the same time that the 'homunculus' himself may be probably disappointed in a speculation. A theatre like the Princess's, possessing so many genuine and legitimate attractions, should be above such low things as dwarfs in either intellect or stature. It may contrive to do very well without them.

Barnum's autobiography gives a differing opinion on the success or otherwise of the exhibition at the theatre and how he then advanced the promotion of Tom Thumb to the public. I think that Barnum had realised, from his experiences in Liverpool and at the Princess's Theatre, that exhibiting Tom Thumb to the general public *en masse* was not the way forward at this time. British society was riddled with a class system that placed the aristocracy and nobility at the top of the pyramid, the Monarchy being the pinnacle. Barnum wanted to tap into this system and to garner patronage for both himself and Stratton. This would be certain to ensure his own social standing and to open doors for him in the future. It is interesting to consider that even today, in Britain, that many organisations, charities, etc., often seek either royal or noble patronage to further their causes. Barnum outlined his next steps;

> The General made so decided a 'hit' at Princess's theatre ... I was offered a much higher figure for a re-engagement, but my purpose had been sufficiently answered. The news was out that General Tom Thumb was on the tapis, as an unparalleled curiosity, and it only remained for me to bring him before the public, 'on my own book', in my own time and way ... From this magnificent mansion [on Grafton Street], I sent letters of invitation to the editors and several of the nobility, to visit the General. Most of them called, and were highly gratified. The word of approval was indeed so passed around in high circles, that uninvited parties drove to my door in crested carriages, and were not admitted. (Barnum 1855)

This turned out to be a very shrewd move by Barnum. Editors of the more respected London newspapers responded to the invitations and gave full reports of their visits, such as here;

> GENERAL TOM THUMB – This diminutive individual, who recently appeared at the Princess's Theatre, has for the past day or two has been receiving visitors, upon special invitation, at the present residence of his guardian, Mr Barnum, in Grafton-street. It is curious to see this vigorous and condensed little creature – as small as if you viewed him through the wrong end of an opera glass – enter the room. He salutes you with the air of a 'well graced actor', and expresses in shrill musical tones his gratification at your visit ... He holds out his hand, and you bury it in yours ... Fashionable too is he in his dress – it must have been made by Queen Mab. There is

the tiny coat with tiny bang-tails, the inch and a half waistcoat, the minikin trowsers (sic), boots that would hardly encase a respectable sized toe, and straps – honest, unflinching straps – to match. A variety of atomy furniture is about him – sofas no longer than a brace of spans, and chairs extinguishable with a hat. There is a little house, too, about the size of the Emperor of Lilliput's palace, into which the *homulus* goes, and looks at you knowingly through the window. Altogether the exhibition is curious ... In short, he is a compressed image of Adam – an incarnate dot – a pocket edition of humanity without abridgements (*London Evening Standard* 2 March 1844)

Clearly Barnum had gone to great lengths to dress these exhibitions to enhance the performance of Stratton. The use of miniature furniture to enhance the stature of a dwarf was something that had been used before (Woolf 2019:45). It was a well-rehearsed theatrical performance for the benefit of a private and specially invited audience. Indeed, the reporter in the above piece was perceptive enough to recognise that Stratton gave the appearance of a 'well graced actor'. Those who attended these exhibitions without an invitation were turned away but Barnum was astute enough to take their visiting cards and then issue them, almost immediately, with an invitation. A continuous stream of nobility and wealthy individuals made their way to the Grafton Street exhibitions over the coming weeks and Barnum's celebrity status was affirmed when he, and Stratton, were invited to attend a private party given by Baroness Rothschild at her mansion in Piccadilly. A carriage was sent for them, and they were ushered into the mansion through the main entrance. They spent around two hours at this party and mixed freely with other Lords and Ladies, thereby raising their social standing even further. On leaving the event, Barnum records that 'an elegant and well-filled purse was quietly slipped into my hand and I felt that the golden shower was beginning to fall!' This was only the first of many such private and illustrious parties to which they would be invited and rewarded. Shortly afterwards an invitation was sent for them to attend a party given by another wealthy banker, Mr Drummond.

Barnum was making progress and his strategy of seeking noble patronage was paying off but the prize of royal patronage still eluded him. When he arrived in Britain he carried with him letters of introduction to Edward Everett from the editor of the *New York Tribune*, Horace Greeley. Everett, an academic and former Congressman had been appointed United States Minister to the Court of St. James in 1841. He was the 'top' American in Britain at the time, and he was well respected by all. Barnum made his acquaintance and presented his letters of introduction. Everett was fascinated by Stratton and invited Barnum and his prodigy to dine with him. Over dinner the matter was raised of a possible audience with Queen Victoria and Everett promised Barnum that he would do what he could to facilitate this. Although he did not have any direct influence over palace matters, he did 'know' people. One of these was the Honourable Charles Augustus Murray, Master of the Queen's Household. Murray was very much sympathetic to America and had previously spent several years travelling widely throughout America, including a significant amount of time with the indigenous native population. After being appointed to the Queen's Household in 1838, he went on to publish an account of his time in America under the title *Travels in North America*. Sometime in March, Barnum and Stratton received an invitation to breakfast with Everett. To this morning meeting Murray had also been invited. Preparing for this meeting, Barnum had ensured that he had read Murray's book and made much of praising him for his interest in America. To add pressure on Murray, Barnum made it clear that a successful audience with the Queen was very necessary to the success of his British visit and, should an audience not be able to be arranged, he would move his small company across to Paris, where he hoped to get an audience with the French king Louise Phillipe. Barnum was playing his trump card! He was well aware of the rivalry between Britain and France, and he felt sure that the British Royal Court would want the *caché* of seeing Tom Thumb before the French Court. The breakfast meeting ended with Murray intimating that something might be able to be arranged.

Barnum had no idea as to whether his request would be agreed to or even how long he would have to wait. Rather than rely totally upon the patronage and reward of the nobility for income, he decided to exhibit Tom Thumb further publicly. Having already achieved celebrity status within noble ranks, with all the press coverage that had generated, it was important to Barnum that people of all ranks should have access to his exhibition. His mixed experiences at the Princess's Theatre led him to believe that a more controlled environment was needed. And accordingly, he rented a room at the Egyptian Hall on Piccadilly. The Egyptian Hall was a well-known suite of exhibition rooms that was opened in 1812 by William Bullock as a venue for his vast collection of natural history and other curiosities. At that time, it was known as the London Museum or Bullock's Museum. It was built in the Egyptian style, the façade appearing as an elaborate temple with giant statues of Isis and Osiris. By 1816, the Hall was used for more general exhibits when hundreds of thousands of people visited an exhibition of Napoleonic memorabilia, including the bullet-proof carriage used by Napoleon that was captured after the Battle of Waterloo. By the time that Barnum rented an upstairs room in the building, Bullock's collections had long since been auctioned off and the Egyptian Hall was being used for more

The Egyptian Hall c.1828 (Public domain image)

general exhibitions of curiosities. In fact, in the main downstairs hall, George Catlin was exhibiting his North American Indian Collection of nine Ojibbeway Indians.

The exhibition opened on the 20th of March;

> GENERAL TOM THUMB – the celebrated AMERICAN DWARF – This interesting and extraordinary phenomenon, will be PUBLICLY exhibited on and after Wednesday, the 20th inst., at the EGYPTIAN HALL, Piccadilly, for a short time only, previous to his departure for Paris ... He receives visitors at his house, 13 Grafton-street, Bond-street, this day only. The General will wait on the nobility and gentry at their residences any night after nine o'clock, after due notice being given (*Morning Herald (London)* 19 March 1844)

General Tom Thumb (Charles S. Stratton) as Napoleon. Daguerreotype c. 1845.

(Barnum Museum. Bridgeport, Connecticut)

Subsequent daily advertisements in several newspapers for the exhibition[5] informed that the 'General' would recite details of his history and education, as well as giving imitations of Napoleon and the Grecian Statues, and songs and dances. Basically, it was the same performance as given at the Princess's Theatre and at Grafton Street, but not as intimate as those at his home or as open to public vulgarity as at the theatre. The hours of exhibition were given as; from Eleven to One, from Three to Five, and from Half past Six to Nine o'clock. Admission prices were 1 shilling for both adults and children. Always open to opportunity, Barnum advertised for many subsequent weeks that the exhibition would shortly close due to the imminent departure of Tom Thumb for Paris. This was a ploy to encourage those who had yet to see the exhibition to do so, and also to encourage those who had already visited but might want to do so again. The exhibitions would actually continue until late July when the Egyptian Hall was put up for auction. At that time, it was reported that the estimated daily income was as much as £125 and that Barnum was outlaying the sum of £44 per month for renting the room[6]. An indication of total ticket numbers for the exhibitions at the Egyptian Hall was given in the *Essex Herald* on the 23rd of July;

General Tom Thumb left London on the 13th inst. [he actually closed his season at the Egyptian Hall on the 20th]. His number of visitors up to that day (counting only the tickets sold) was 194,699, and adding those at public exhibitions the number is calculated at about 300,000. He has purchased an elegant pair of ponies and has ordered a splendid equipage corresponding with his size.

If this figure is correct, at 1 shilling per entry, Barnum's estimated income for the Egyptian Hall season only would have amounted to £15,000 [over £900,000 equivalent today]! Not only was Barnum drawing in the money through entrance fees, but he was also still exploiting handsome rewards from the nobility and other wealthy persons. The General now demanded the trappings of a gentleman, and that included a diminutive carriage.

GENERAL TOM THUMB'S EQUIPAGE

> The career of the miniature hero, Tom Thumb, in this country, has been one unvaried round of success; and if proof were wanted of the sterling results, it must be adduced in the fact that he now possesses the outward and visible attribute of a gentleman – he keeps his carriage. Mr S. Beaton, of No. 16 Denmark-street, Soho, has just built for his Generalship an elegant dress chariot, suitable to the dimensions of the hero (*Illustrated London News* 31 August 1844)

General Tom Thumb's carriage (Illustrated London News *31 August 1844)*

Barnum must have outlaid a significant amount of money for Stratton's carriage because a later description of it shows how ostentatious it may have looked;

> ... complete in all its parts – even to springs, window blinds, and folding steps, and quite available to the purposes of locomotion. It is a chariot about $3^{1/2}$ feet in height; the body is of intense blue, and the mouldings are of silver, the wheels are elegantly picked out with white, the hammer-cloth is of rich crimson, embroidered fancifully, containing also the General's arms, a mixture of the heraldic symbols of England and America, with the business-like recommendation 'Go a-head' flourishing underneath in the form of a motto ... Two small boys have been obtained to fill the arduous situations of coachman and footman (*Royal Cornwall Gazette* 6 September 1844)

All of Barnum's efforts and expenses were soon to pay off and he was shortly to achieve his principal ambition of presenting General Tom Thumb to the court of Queen Victoria.

Notes

1   Register of Passports 1843 – 1846. National Archives and Records Administration.

2   The American War of 1812.

3   Prevention of Cruelty to and Protection of Children Bill. (No. 372). HC Deb 14 August 1889 vol 339 cc1284-7 Online at; Prevention of Cruelty to and Protection of Children Bill. (No. 372). (Hansard, 14 August 1889) (parliament.uk).

4   Brobdignag was a fictional land populated by giants and was featured in the satirical novel Gulliver's *Travels* (1726) by Jonathan Swift.

5   *Morning Herald (London)* 20 March 1844.

6   *Bells' Weekly Messenger* 27 July 1844.

CHAPTER 4 – A ROYAL SEAL OF APPROVAL

On Saturday the 23rd of March a placard appeared on the door of the Egyptian Hall. It read; 'Closed this evening, General Tom Thumb being at Buckingham Palace by command of Her Majesty'. Murray had been true to his word and an audience with the Queen had been arranged for Barnum and Stratton. His ambition had been achieved! Barnum records this in his autobiography;

> ...one of the Life Guards, a tall noble-looking fellow, bedecked as became his station, brought me a note, conveying the Queen's invitation to General Tom Thumb and his guardian, Mr Barnum, to appear at Buckingham Palace on an evening specified. Special instructions were the same day orally given by Mr Murray, by Her Majesty's command, to suffer the General to appear before her, as he would appear anywhere else, without any training in the use of the titles of royalty, as the Queen desired to see him act naturally and without restraint ... We were conducted through a long corridor to a broad flight of marble steps, which led to the Queen's magnificent picture gallery, where Her Majesty and Prince Albert, the Duchess of Kent, and twenty or thirty of the nobility, were awaiting our arrival. They were standing at the farther end of the room when the doors were thrown open and the General toddled in, looking like a wax-doll gifted with the power of locomotion. (Barnum 1855)

Barnum goes on to explain how both he and the General were instructed in the correct protocols for meeting with royalty, bowing in a certain manner and not speaking directly to the Queen but through an intermediary. From personal experience, I know myself how difficult it is to focus on these protocols when being presented to royalty, so it is hardly surprising that both visitors made some slips, but these seem to have been overlooked. All of the London newspapers on the following Monday morning carried this note;

> The Royal dinner party, at Buckingham Palace, on Saturday evening, included Her Royal Highness the Duchess of Kent, Lady Anna Maria Dawson, the Earl of Liverpool, the Earl of Aberdeen, Mr George Edward, and the Hon. Mrs Anson.

> The American dwarf, General Tom Thumb, accompanied by his guardian, Mr P T Barnum, of New York, had the honour of attending at the Palace in the evening, where the General exhibited his clever imitations of Napoleon, &c., which elicited the approbation of Her Majesty and the Royal circle (*Morning Post* 25 March 1844)

Queen Victoria made an entry about the visit into her personal journal;

> After dinner we saw the greatest curiosity, I, or indeed anybody ever saw, viz: a little dwarf, only 25 inches high & 15 lb in weight. No description can give an idea of this little creature, whose real name was Charles Stratton, born they say in 32 [1832], which makes him 12 years old. He is American, & gave us his card, with Gen: Tom Thumb, written on it. He made the funniest little bow, putting out his hand & saying: 'much obliged Mama'. One cannot help feeling

very sorry for the poor little thing & wishing he could be properly cared for, for the people who show him off tease him a good deal, I should think. He was made to imitate Napoleon & do all parts of tricks, finally, backing out the whole way out of the Gallery[1].

It is interesting to note that the Queen appeared to display some empathy towards the situation of Stratton. The implication is that she recognised that he was being exploited by 'the people who show him off'. At that time, Queen Victoria was still a young married woman of 25 years. She also had three young children, Victoria aged three and a half, Albert aged two and a half, and Alice aged almost one year. She was also pregnant with her fourth child, Alfred. It would seem only natural for her to display a maternal instinct towards the young Stratton.

Barnum was now able to capitalise on his audience with the Queen. He could now say 'as seen by Her Majesty Queen Victoria' in his

advertising. Public awareness of this royal patronage would have generated a larger audience response to the exhibitions. During Victoria's reign the behaviour of the royal family, especially that of the Queen, very much influenced the behaviour of the general public. This is all bound up in the class system,

*Tom Thumb visits Queen Victoria and Prince Albert, with the Duke of Wellington behind (*The Pictorial Times *13 April 1844)*

where the 'lower classes' looked up to and emulated their betters. If the Queen was to see Tom Thumb, then why not should they? This may be a very British phenomenon. Although the class system may not be as rigid and the monarchy may have less support than in Victoria's time, the fashions and behaviour of the royal family can still have an influence on how people behave. As I write this in early 2024, King Charles III has recently been in hospital for prostate treatment. It has been reported that websites concerned with prostate problems have seen an increased volume of traffic. On the day after news of his diagnosis was released in the media there were 16,410 visits to the National Health Service prostate website compared to 1,414 on the previous day. If the Princess of Wales appears in a new fashionable outfit, it is not long before there is a demand on the high street for that style of clothing. In Barnum's case, Queen Victoria's patronage equalled more people 'through the door'. It also brought about further royal invitations. Within a week of visiting the palace, Barnum and Stratton had been summoned to give an exhibition before Her Majesty the Queen Dowager [Queen Victoria's aunt] at Marlborough House, on The Mall.

Fortune seemed to favour Barnum for he soon received a second invitation to attend Buckingham Palace on the 1st of April. Why the Queen should have requested a further visit is never recorded and, indeed, she only makes a passing reference to the visit in her journal[2].

> Saw the little dwarf, in the Yellow Drawingroom, who was very nice, lively, and funny, dancing & singing wonderfully. Vicky & Bertie were with us, also Mama, L[y] Dunmore, & her 3 children, & L[y] Lyttleton. Little 'Tom Thumb' does not reach up to Vicky's shoulder.

In the above, Vicky and Bertie refer to her two eldest children Victoria and Albert; Mama was Victoria, the Duchess of Kent; Lady Dunmore was Lady of the Bedchamber to Queen Victoria; and Lady Lyttleton was Governess to the royal children. It is of course possible that the Queen merely wished her children to meet Barnum and Tom Thumb. If her journal recorded very little of the visit, then the London newspapers were more expansive;

> Last night, pursuant to the commands of Her Majesty, 'General Tom Thumb', the celebrated American dwarf, had the honour of appearing, for the second time, before the Court at Buckingham Palace ... In addition to her Majesty the Queen, her Majesty the Queen of the Belgians, his Royal Highness the Prince of Wales [Albert], the Princess Royal [Victoria], the Princess Alice, and their respective suites, a distinguished party had been invited to witness the performance of this extraordinary specimen of mankind ... Her Majesty the Queen, at the conclusion of the entertainment, was pleased to present to the General, with her own hand, a superb souvenir, of the most exquisite handicraft, manufactured of mother-of-pearl, and mounted with gold and precious stones. On one side are the Crown and Royal initials 'V.R.', and on the reverse bouquets of flowers in enamel and rubies. In addition to this splendid gift her Majesty subsequently presented the General with a beautiful gold pencil-case, with the initials of Tom Thumb, and his coat of arms engraved on the emerald surmounting the case, accompanying the Royal souvenir with the expression of her Majesty's high gratification at the versatile talents of the General, and also a compliment to Mr Barnum, his guardian, on the aptness of his pupil (*London Evening Standard* 2 April 1844)

On returning to the Egyptian Hall for the afternoon exhibition, Barnum immediately placed the Royal gifts, and any other gifts that Stratton had received, on display. This aroused even further curiosity and awe in the visiting public. Not long after the exhibition opened, another very notable figure paid a visit. The article above continues;

The dwarf had scarcely made his appearance in the afternoon at the Egyptian Hall, when his Grace the Duke of Wellington honoured the General with a visit. At the moment the Duke entered the room the General was in the act of giving an imitation of Napoleon musing at St. Helena; and on the hero of Waterloo inquiring of Mr Barnum what the General was meditating upon, Mr Barnum happily [and perhaps with quick-thinking] replied, 'Upon the loss of the battle of Waterloo'. His Grace then took the dwarf into his arms, and asked him several questions, with the answer to which the Duke appeared much pleased. On his departure the Duke presented the General with a handsome present.

Another gift to be added to the public display! Barnum and Stratton were now moving in illustrious circles and their popularity continued— but not in all circles. Some newspaper reports were more critical of the royal attention feted upon them.

TOM THUMB AND THE QUEEN - Her Majesty has again commanded 'the performances of Tom Thumb, the Yankee Dwarf'. This, indeed, was to be expected. We had only to reflect upon the countless acts of patronage towards the arts and sciences – had only to remember a few of the numerous personal condescensions of the Queen towards men of letters, artists, and philosophers – to be assured that even Tom Thumb would be welcomed with that graceful cordiality which has heretofore made Buckingham Palace and Windsor Castle the homes of poetry and science. *De minimis curat Regina*! [the Queen takes care of the smallest things] Continental monarchs stop short in their royal favours at full grown authors and artists; but the enthusiasm of Her Majesty Queen Victoria ... lavishes with prodigal hand the most delicate honours upon an American Tom Thumb, whose astounding genius it is to measure in his boots five-and -twenty inches! ... Tom Thumb being – according to the biography published by his showman, Barnum – the son of a Yankee carpenter, we should much like to know the General's arms. Did her Majesty, before the 'performance', send to learn them, that they might be duly engraved; or were they ... struck off in a 'moment of enthusiasm'? ... Touching the royal gifts presented by the Queen to Tom Thumb, Mr Barnum, the showman, has, in the handsomest manner, offered them, as additional objects of attraction, to a certain exhibition about to be opened to the public (*Cork Examiner* 17 April 1844)

Although blatantly critical, and somewhat anti-American in sentiment, the article does raise an interesting question. Exactly what was the coat of arms engraved on the gift that he had been given? Perhaps they were the ones created for him later to appear on the side of his diminutive carriage. The theme is taken up by the *Satirist* of the 5th of May;

If it should happen, for instance, that her Majesty Queen Victoria has no sort of liking for the conversation of wits, poets, painters (portrait-painters excepted), and men of genius in general, but should display a decided taste for petting of parrots, puppies, marmosets, monkeys, and living monstrosities in general, so much the worse for herself, not for us ... there is no mistake about the patronage bestowed on General Tom Thumb. Whether she has done much or nothing at all for great men, there is no disputing her enthusiasm for little ones ... when do we hear of any man of real talent being commanded to show himself three times before his sovereign? Once is quite enough, even if by any lucky chance he gains the honour of an interview. Historians, dramatists, sculptors and men of learning do not get gold watches, ordered expressly for them, nor, as far as we know, are costly tokens of respect showered among them through the bounty or caprice of her Majesty ... Thus petted by royalty, and patronised by the queen Dowager ... Who can wonder either, that he is in a fair way of making a fortune, either for himself or for his guardian, Mr Barnum?

But all press coverage is good publicity and in his advertising for the Tom Thumb exhibition, Barnum now lead with 'under the especial Patronage of her Most Gracious Majesty the Queen, H.R.H. Prince Albert, the Queen Dowager, H.R.H. the Duchess of Kent, and the Queen of the Belgians'[3]. Gifts from royalty continued to be showered on them. A miniature gold watch and chain was presented to Tom Thumb by the Queen Dowager on his second invitation to attend Marlborough House on the 17th of April. He attended in full court dress, complete with sword and buckles. At this event the Duchess of Gloucester and the Duke of Cambridge were also in attendance. Then came the unprecedented third invitation to attend Buckingham Palace. By now both Barnum and Stratton were familiar with palace protocol and quite at home in mixing with royalty and nobility. The *St James's Chronicle* reported that 'On the entrance of Tom Thumb, he was received by her majesty with all the familiarity of an old acquaintance'[4]. Queen Victoria only makes a passing reference in her journal for that day.

*Tom Thumb in court dress (*The Pictorial Times *27 December 1845)*

On his [Prince Albert] return at 6, we all saw the dwarf, whom our guests were much surprised at. He appeared in different costumes. [5]

It is interesting that the references seem to get shorter each time he visited the palace. Could it have been that her Majesty's interest in Tom Thumb was waning and she had only invited him to present to her guests? Another satirical attack on the visit was made by the *Punch* magazine, printed in early May;

PRIVATE THEATRICALS AT BUCKINGHAM PALACE - The farce of Tom Thumb was repeated on Friday afternoon for the third time, at Buckingham Palace. Tom Thumb enacted his original character, supported by the King of the Belgians, as Noodle, his Serene Highness the Prince of Leiningen taking the insignificant part of Doodle. The prologue was spoken by Mr Barnum, the showman, disguised as a guardian. At the end of the performance, Tom Thumb made his well-known bow, by Her Majesty's command, and favoured the royal party with some gratuitous remarks on the furniture, which were not quite so successful (*Leeds Times* 4 May 1844)

Although Barnum may have been happy to have had Tom Thumb constantly in the news, there was a sense that perhaps 'Tom Thumb mania' was beginning to wane. Although the exhibitions at the Egyptian Hall, and later at the Adelaide Gallery, continued for a few more weeks, had they reached saturation point in the metropolis? After all, there were only so many times that people would want to pay to see Tom Thumb give a repetitious performance and even the nobility would eventually exhaust their interest. Tom Thumb was becoming something of a one trick pony in some people's eyes. Critical comments, like the ones given above, would not have helped the overall situation. This was the opportune time to move out of London and take Tom Thumb to people in the provinces. But we should not forget that one of the other missions of Barnum's visit to Britain and Europe was to scout new curiosities for his museum back in New York. Whilst most of his efforts had been tied up in promoting Tom Thumb he did, at times, secure novelties to be sent back to America. As early as March it was reported;

GREAT AND SMALL CURIOSITIES – An immense giant and giantess, and a very diminutive dwarf, sailed in the ship Yorkshire, yesterday, for New York. As Mr Barnum and Mr Barnett, managers of the New York Museum, are both scouring Europe for curiosities, we expect these are sent by one of those gentlemen *(Leeds Intelligencer* 9 March 1844)

And later, in April;

COSMORAMA ROOMS – We have now at these rooms a pair of babes, scarcely emerged from the cradle, entertaining such of the public as choose to visit them with songs and dances. These miniature performers are anonymous, simply going by the appellation of the 'infant sisters' and infantine they indeed are. The youngest, about four years old is the singer ...The second 'infant' is a year or two older, a little taller, and with a much more available cleverness. She is the dancer ... We learn that these infantine prodigies have been engaged for America by Mr Barnum, the guardian of Tom Thumb, where they will appear at his American Museum, in New York, on their arrival per steamer *(Age (London)* 27 April 1844)

Barnum's lease on the room at the Egyptian Hall expired towards the end of July and this became the moment when he would venture further afield. Had his London season been a success? The following piece would seem to confirm so;

GENERAL TOM THUMB closes his exhibition in London today, after which he proceeds to several of the most important provincial towns, Ireland, Scotland, and France. The General opened his exhibition at the Egyptian Hall on the 20th March last, and thus he will have remained in London four consecutive months. The number of his visitors up to Saturday night last (counting only the tickets sold) was 194,699, being an average of over 2,000 per day, besides which he has during the same time exhibited four nights at the Princess's theatre, four times at the Royal Surrey Zoological Gardens, at the Surrey theatre, and other public institutions, twenty-four nights at the Royal Adelaide Gallery—thus increasing the number of his auditors to about 300,000. How many ladies the little gentleman has kissed out of the number we would hardly dare guess. The General has been three times before Her Majesty, twice before the Queen Dowager (from both of whom he received valuable presents), and once before the Duchess of Kent and the King and Queen of the Belgians. He has been visited by the Dukes of Cambridge, Wellington, Devonshire, Buckingham, Bedford, and, in fact, by nearly all the nobility of England, as well as the Foreign Ministers, Officers of State &c. He has visited many of their mansions, and received a host of presents from persons of the highest distinction. The General has purchased an elegant pair of ponies, and has ordered a splendid equipage, corresponding in size with himself; it has been building for several months, and will be completed in about three weeks, when the General will return to London to take possession of it, but will remain here only three or four days (*Age (London)* 20 July 1844)

Barnum must have been extremely pleased with this illustrious resumé of his time in London, but now was the time to move on. Apart from a few days in London in early August, Barnum took the Tom Thumb show on the road for the rest of the month, visiting the major towns and cities of Britain.

The General will be in Bath on August 12th, 13th, 14th, and 15th: Bristol 16th, 17th, 19th, 20th, and 21st: Glocester [sic] 22d:

*The Adelaide Gallery (*The Pictorial Times *13 April 1844)*

Cheltenham 23d to 29th: Leamington 30th and 31st, and September 2d: Birmingham September 4th to 9th: Manchester 10th to 23d: Liverpool 24th to 30th: and then proceed north to the largest provincial towns – Edinburgh, Glasgow, Dublin &c (*The Times* 26 July 1844)

In fact, during the latter half of the year, Barnum and Stratton criss-crossed the country from east to west and north to south, often revisiting towns that they had already appeared in. That October, Barnum returned briefly to New York to oversee matters concerning his American Museum. He also took the opportunity of collecting his wife and two surviving daughters for his return to Britain in November. He had been away from home too long and wished to have them with him.

Disaster almost struck on the 18th of August near Clifton, Bristol, when the carriage in which the party were travelling crashed into a high stone wall. The horse was killed instantly. Stratton and his tutor, Mr Sherman, were travelling on the driver's box and were thrown from the carriage. At the moment of impact, Sherman grabbed Stratton in his arms and leapt clear across the nine-foot-high wall, landing safely in an adjacent field. Barnum and Stratton's father were travelling inside and received a few cuts and bruises but were otherwise unscathed. Although they feared that their companions had been crushed by the horse and carriage, their fears were unfounded when the two appeared unharmed. Barnum gifted 100 guineas as a reward to Sherman for his quick thinking.

Wherever they appeared, as in London, they were showered with gifts. In Birmingham, Stratton was even presented with a miniature working firearm, manufactured in the gun shops of the city. This was added to the growing collection of gifts put on display. Now that Stratton had his tiny equipage, this accompanied him everywhere. Sometimes, on visiting a town, as here in Birmingham, he would process through the streets in it or otherwise appear on stage with it.

> ... whilst in the coffee-room [we] were disturbed by an unwonted tumult and hum of voices in the street, whereon some of the windows looked. There was also a similar riot in the yard; and in both places we found some three or four hundred people assembled, in eager expectation apparently of seeing something wonderful. The mystery was soon solved. Two grooms opened the doors of a coach-house with important gravity; the boys set up a great shout, and the Lilliputian carriage of *General Tom Thumb*, with its pygmy ponies, coachmen, and lacquey, drove out into the street, amidst the turbulent cheers of the spectators. We found the small 'General' was sojourning in our hotel; and that his equipage paraded the principal

streets two or three times a day, as an advertisement (*Railway Bell and London Advertiser* 14 September 1844)

*General Tom Thumb standing between P T Barnum and his wife Charity (*Country Life *27 September 1956)*

By November, the tour had made its way to Scotland and appeared several times in both Glasgow and Edinburgh. While appearing in Edinburgh, Stratton was presented with a full set of Highland dress. From this point onwards it became an integral part of his exhibitions as Tom Thumb made his appearance as a Highland chief. By early December, the group had made its way to Belfast and then on to Dublin, but controversy was to follow them. It had not escaped the attention of the Tax Office that a great deal of money was being made on this tour.

GENERAL TOM THUMB AND THE INCOME TAX COMMISSIONERS – The 'general, while exhibiting in Glasgow (which city he has lately left for Dublin), received, shortly before his departure, a visit from an official, who, to his great surprise, presented him, by order of the commissioners of the Income-tax for Glasgow, with a printed form to be filled up, calling him to make a return of the amount of his income derivable by the exhibition of his diminutive person ... The Scotch commissioners have now pursued the little general to Dublin, and having assumed that his annual receipts are 25,000*l* [pounds sterling], have assessed him to that amount, and now call on him for 729*l* [pounds sterling] towards the Income tax. This demand Mr Barnum resists (*Morning Post* 21 December 1844)

Barnum's argument was that as a non-British resident neither he nor Stratton were liable to pay British income tax. The issue rumbled on for several months, until March 1845, when it was reported briefly that;

General Tom Thumb (an American), through his guardian, has been compelled to pay his quota to the Income Tax (*Sussex Advertiser* 18 March 1845)

The implication of this is that Stratton, through Barnum, did eventually pay the sum demanded. Strangely, Barnum makes no reference to this matter at all in his autobiography.

On their return from Ireland, they continued the tour of Britain visiting some towns on both the south and east coast that they had not already visited. Stratton even found time to present his Tom Thumb at Astley's Royal Amphitheatre in London. This was the very home of circus in Britain, which had been founded by Philip Astley at the end of the eighteenth century. Here Stratton played for two consecutive nights. It is interesting to note that Wales was never included in the tour of Britain. Barnum never mentions the country and one wonders as to why the good ladies of Wales were never given the opportunity to kiss the General's lips.

Although Tom Thumb was generally well received throughout the tour, there were occasions when the behaviour of Stratton, as Tom

Advertising flyer for General Tom Thumb c.1846 (Author's collection)

Thumb, were frowned upon. One of these incidents revolves around the issue of Stratton demanding a kiss from the ladies as payment; and he is reported to have kissed thousands of ladies both in America and Britain. Barnum clearly sanctioned this behaviour and one must wonder as to his reasoning. He was presenting a seven/eight-year-old child as an 11/12-year-old who was, in essence, portraying his character as a young gentleman of older years. What were the ladies seeing when they saw Tom Thumb? Did they see the reality of a child or did they see a miniature man?

Did they want to 'mother' him or was there a deeper psychosexual element at play? Did Barnum recognise that some women might have, what today, is termed SIC (sexual interest in children) and capitalise on it by encouraging lip-kissing, an intimate, and sexually charged, form of contact? This does not mean that these were women who had paedophilic tendencies but it is a notably strange phenomenon. In a 2023 study[6] concerning women with a sexual interest in children, some of the participants stated that 'I found boys/young men beautiful' or 'I envy the beautiful way that children see the world without sexuality clouding their vision. I hate the adult world for trying to pervert them. I want to be a child again ...' This is a very complex area of study and one that is far beyond the scope of this book—but the matter of Tom Thumb frequently kissing ladies' lips did become an issue from time to time. An article appeared in the *Buxton Herald* regarding an exhibition in Worcester. It was prompted by a letter to the *Worcester Journal* from a man who signed himself as 'The Father of the Family'. It is rather lengthy but worthy of reading:

The song finished, the little monkey [Tom Thumb] was furnished with some books (his life), and prints of himself, which he proceeded to sell at a shilling, giving to each lady purchaser a kiss, being what he called a 'stamped receipt'; and it made me disgusted with my own inches to see with what rapidity the creature got rid of his wares; in a moment there were a hundred hands, each with a shilling, and as many mouths, each eager for a kiss stretched towards him; there was the flushed and warm-faced young lady and the parchment-visaged old one, the fair and demure Baptist, and severe Independent, and the poke-bonneted Quakeress, all with protruded lips, sucking in his kisses at a shilling each, tempting one to start the mathematical question at every moment ... Master Tommy came round to our part of the table, squeaking 'Buy my book.' 'Give me a shilling' said my wife. 'For what?' I demanded. 'For a book'. 'Rather say a kiss' said I. 'Well. A kiss then, if you like.' 'Pshaw, my dear, you can have one nearer home for nothing, or, if your taste takes a diminutive turn, you can kiss all and each of your seven children gratis, as often as you like, and have the additional reflection that you are sparing their papa's pocket into the bargain.' 'Buy my book; come, be lively' squeaked Thomas once more. 'Make haste, the shilling, my love' reiterated my wife, and, suiting word to action, she placed her finger in my waistcoat pocket, and in a moment more, my twelvepenny token was paid over to a dwarf for a kiss by the mother of my seven children! 'Alright' added the little abortion to the tall Yankee [Barnum]. 'Look lively, ladies' and my daughters did so, but it was towards me. They wanted their shilling's worth too; I felt it would be unjust to refuse them the luxury their mother hankered for before their eyes (*Buxton Herald* 7 September 1844)

The lead to the article claims that Stratton raised £110 at that exhibition. If every shilling taken was from a woman and returned with a kiss that would mean 2,200 kisses! Of course, there would have been men who

Entry token for general Tom Thumb exhibition c.1846 (Image courtesy Thom Wall)

would have bought the book so it is unlikely that so many kisses were given but no doubt there were many! The letter writer certainly airs his disgust and creates a somewhat 'sleazy' picture and, remember, these were not just peck-on-the-cheek type kisses; they were full blown lip-on-lip kisses. I try to equate Stratton's behaviour with my own grandchildren, who are of a similar age. The 10 and 11-year-old boys would throw their hands up in horror and run if anyone attempted to kiss them on the lips. Even suggesting that they could earn a shilling, or its equivalent today, for a kiss would not tempt them. Although attitudes towards children (and children towards adults) have changed since the Victorian era, Stratton's (and by association Barnum's) behaviour does seem dubious. However, Tom Thumb's appeal to the ladies elicited all sorts of responses—even poetry, as here in the *Bath Chronicle and Weekly Gazette* of 30 January 1845;

LINES TO TOM THUMB
On his appearance at Bath, January 1845

Charming sprite! Bewitching creature,
Unique in ev'ry form and feature,
Your gentle tread we scarce can hear,

And only see you when you're near;
From Lilliput you must have come,
You great, great wonder, little Thumb.
Your fairy hands with jewell'd rings,
Indeed, are 'first rate, 'spicy' things;
The ladies like your 'stamp receipt',
And all pronounce it very sweet.
Your arch expression, roguish eye,
Descriptive powers almost defy:
Your attitudes, so well defin'd,
The Grecian Statues bring to mind;
And well, indeed, you personate
Napoleon too, and imitate
His taking snuff so wondrous well,
We know not where you most excel,
When pond'ring over Waterloo,
Or when King George we see in you,
Or Highland Chieftain, dress'd complete,
With tartan hose and buckled feet;
A claymore in your tiny hand,
And brace of pistols in your band;
But this I know – you're excellent
In ev'ry form you represent;
Though most I like you in your own,
Unrivall'd in your little growth,
To see you bigger all are loth;
You look so pretty as you are,
From the new world a shining star,
Attracting thousands to the sight,
Who all express unfeigned delight.
In sense and goodness only grow,
For they will make you truly great,
Though to be little is your fate;
But may your cares be little too,
And so, dear little man, adieu.

A LADY ADMIRER

Barnum had, through Charles Stratton, created the character of Tom
Thumb with utter success. The tour so far had been a total success. He

had visited almost every part of Britain and exhibited to thousands of people. He had been fêted by royalty and the nobility. Tom Thumb had kissed, in his own claim, 'two millions of ladies' and had moved women to poetry. His likeness was on display in Madame Tussaud's Wax Works and had been sold as dolls and portraits. He had inspired rivals and imitators, some of them female. There was even a comic pantomime produced in January 1845 that bore his name. With all this success behind him, how would they be received in France?

Notes

1   *Queen Victoria's Journals.* Princess Beatrice's copies. Saturday 23rd March 1844. Online at; Queen Victoria's Journals - Journal Entry (queenvictoriasjournals.org) Vol.17 (1st January 1844 – 31st July 1844) Vol. page 93_

2   *Queen Victoria's Journals.* Princess Beatrice's copies. Monday 1st April 1844. Online at; Queen Victoria's Journals - Journal Entry (queenvictoriasjournals. org) Vol.17 (1st January 1844 – 31st July 1844) Vol. page 102

3   *Morning Herald (London)* 18 April 1844.

4   *St James's Chronicle* 20 April 1844. The story of Tom Thumb and the Queen's poodle is only ever mentioned by Barnum in his autobiography. No mention of the incident was made in any of the news reports of the visit to Buckingham Palace. Certainly, Queen Victoria did not mention it in her journal. There is an engraving of the occasion held by the Barnum Museum that appears in the Select illustrations from the book; 'Life of Barnum' (published 1881). Online at https://ctdigitalarchive.org/node/112174. The same engraving appeared in the *Sketch of the Life, Personal Appearance, Character and Manners of Charles S. Stratton.* This was published in New York in 1863 by Wynkoop & Hallenbeck, 19 years after the event.

5   *Queen Victoria's Journals.* Princess Beatrice's copies. Friday 19th April 1844. Online at; Queen Victoria's Journals - Journal Entry (queenvictoriasjournals. org) Vol.17 (1st January 1844 – 31st July 1844) Vol. page 123.

6   Tozdan, S., Hübener, G., Briken, P. *et al.* (2023) *What do women with sexual interest in children tell us about the assumed cause of their sexual interest in children, (non)disclosure, and professional help?—Results of a qualitative content analysis. International Journal of Impotence Research* (2023). Online at https://doi.org/10.1038/s41443-023-00677-6

CHAPTER 5 – VIVE LA FRANCE

After a whirlwind successful tour of Great Britain, Barnum and his entourage set sail for continental Europe in the spring of 1845. The tour was to commence in Paris, where he hoped to be as successful as in London, and then to progress throughout all of France. Naturally, having been received by Queen Victoria on three occasions, Barnum had eyes on meeting the French court as well. He was not to be disappointed. The French press, notably the *Journal des Debats* gave a lengthy report of the meeting in the issue of 26 March, which was translated and subsequently printed in English in the *Morning Post* of 28 March;

TOM THUMB AT THE TUILERIES

The evening before last at eight o'clock, Tom Thumb was presented to the King and Royal Family [of France]. As may easily be supposed, neither the young Duke of Wurtemburg, the little Duke de Chartres, nor the Count de Paris, was absent from such a *fête*. The dwarf arrived with his suite like a *grand seigneur*. A preceptor, an interpreter, a *valet de chambre*, and a pianist, composed his cortege ... When Tom Thumb entered his Majesty's drawing-room, he was dressed as a 'gentleman', black coat and trousers, shoes and silk stockings, a long cravat flowing over a white waist-coat, and connected with the shirt by a brilliant brooch. Instead of a hat he wore a sailor's casquette[1] ... Tom Thumb is an *aimable* and *gracieux* child, ever smiling and ever anxious to obey the slightest gestures of his guides ... We saw him but once in ill humour. His *valet de chambres* had forgotten in a change of costume one of the necessary articles of his *toilette*. He forgives no such oversight ... He has his pockets crammed with trinkets and microscopic snuff boxes which the inconceivable idolatry of the English women for this child has had made for him. Fanny Ellsler[2] gave him a brooch, which fastened his cravat. Above all, the Queen of England has overwhelmed him with presents. He showed to the King a card case, a gift of her Britannic Majesty, and drew from it a dozen cards of Lilliputian size, which he most gallantly distributed to the Royal Family, commencing by the King, the Queen, the Duchess of Orleans, and ending by the Duke de Chartres ... Everyone remarked the style in which he bowed to the company after some well-applauded exercise; and when he left the Royal drawing-room he retired backwards, in order to present but his face to the august company, conformably to the strict law of diplomatic *etiquette*. The King himself handed to the courteous myrmidon a very handsome diamond brooch, but which was not proportioned to his size; he might have used it as a sword. Nevertheless, the General expressed the wish of thrusting it into his cravat, which he did, by detaching Fanny Essler's brooch ... Tom Thumb concluded his *soirée* at the Tuileries by a very brilliant exhibition of the Scotch costume ... This costume is decidedly the General's triumph ... We therefore advise you to go and see him.

It seemed that all things were set for another triumphant tour. Certainly, he had impressed the Royal court, and left with even more gifts! Strangely in the report, Barnum is not mentioned by name, which is peculiar as Barnum used the opportunity to approach the King, requesting that Tom Thumb be permitted to drive his carriage in the Longchamps celebration. This was an annual event that originated with a Queen's

Advertising poster for General Tom Thumb at the Salle Vivienne in Paris 1845
(Bibliotèque National Français BnF Paris)

yearly religious pilgrimage to a favourite sanctuary. By this time, it had been transformed into an exhibition of open carriages and sleek horses; of silks and satins, of plumes and feathers. It was a celebration of the current fashions. Barnum requested that Tom Thumb drive in the avenue reserved for court carriages. This would avoid any potential damage or harm to the little General by the press of the crowds. The King was only too pleased to grant this request and accordingly this was granted. Although the weather had turned milder and a large crowd had turned out to view the processions on the Champs-Elysée it was reported that the new fashions were unremarkable and that had not Tom Thumb, escorted by a detachment of Municipal Horse Guards, been present there would have been nothing worth looking at[3]. However, Barnum had cleverly inserted his protégé into the fashionable parade of the season and his very presence excited the crowd enough for them to visit his exhibition, which opened at the Salle Vivienne in Paris.

LÉ GÉNÉRAL TOM-POUCE À PARIS
DANS LE PETIT POUCET.

Quadrille pour Piano

Cover image of a musical score for a piano quadrille 1845 (BnF Paris)

General Tom Thumb became an instant hit in Paris. The first day's takings were given as 5,500 Francs and statuettes and pictures of him began to appear in plenty. There were songs written about him, dances composed, and even hats created[4]. There was even a café named Tom Thumb which opened near the Salle Vivienne. Barnum advertised Tom Thumb by his translated French name of Tom Pouce. This created something of a stir as the Theatre des Variétés put up advertising placards for a performance of a dramatic piece entitled 'Tom Pouce'. Edward Stratton, Tom Thumb's father, made an appeal to the Tribunal of Commerce to prevent the manager of the theatre from using that name and demanded damages in the sum of 2,000 Francs for each offence. The manager as defendant argued that;

The plaintiff, being a foreigner, could not plead; That the name of Tom Pouce, like that of Petit Poucet, belonged to anyone that chose to take it; that it could be made the subject of a vaudeville; and that no confusion could arise between the piece at the Variétés and the miniature man at the Concerts Vivienne, since the bills announced that the part of Tom Pouce was to be filled by the little Duhamel. The Tribunal rejected these arguments and declared that the defendant must remove from the bills the name of 'Tom Pouce' and pay all the cost of the suit. The piece at the Variétés has since been advertised under the name of 'Tom Pouff' (*Globe* 28 April 1845)

A success that one might have expected Barnum to applaud in terms of advertising. But it seems he did not capitalise on this at all. Did he deliberately keep his name out of the potential lawsuit for propriety or did he feel that the senior Stratton was better and perhaps more favourably placed as father to make the appeal? This does seem odd, as Barnum was never one to shy away from publicity—of any kind.

But for all that the little General was a hit with most Parisians, there were some sensitive citizens who felt offended by his portrayal of Napoleon. They were under the impression that he had been sent over from England to cast ridicule on the memory of their deceased Emperor[5]. Perhaps Tom Thumb—and Barnum—should have been more discrete! In addition to giving his exhibition at the Salle Vivienne, Barnum had engaged the Theatre de Vaudeville for performances of 'Tom Pouce' in the evenings. But by the end of May his attraction was beginning to wane. It was reported that there had been too much of him and that people were beginning to cry out about his ugliness—he was becoming somewhat of a bore. Barnum and his protégé had made a good living

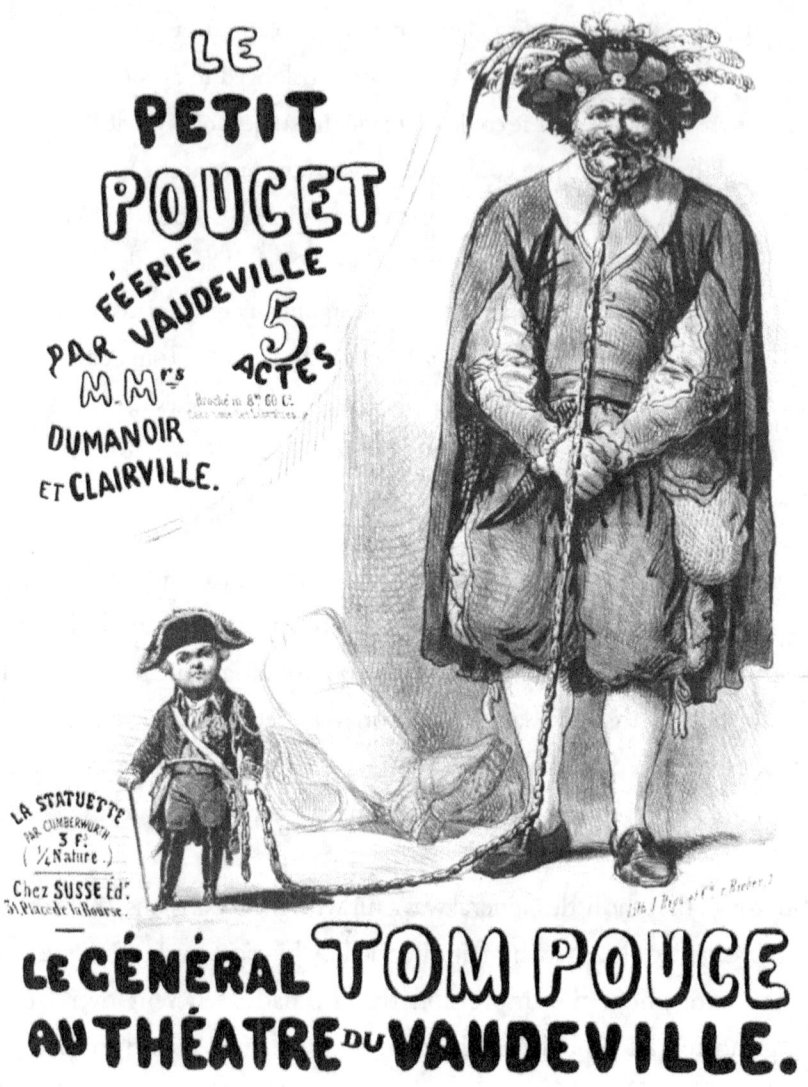

Advertising poster for Tom Thumb at the Théatre du Vaudeville Paris 1845 (BnF Paris)

in Paris but now it was time to take the tour on the road. By early July, Barnum and company made their way to Brussels, Belgium via Rouen and Amiens. The first visit in the capital city was a summons to the King and Queen of the Belgians. They had met Tom Thumb previously in London but wished their children and the Court to meet him. After the

Royal visit the General began to exhibit in the city. Their stay in Brussels was not without mishap. This was to be the beginning of an exhausting tour through continental Europe.

At Rouen, during the eight days of his residence, the spacious saloon in which he appeared every forenoon, was crowded; while the theatre in which he performed in a piece adapted to his peculiar powers[6], was literally wedged every night, although the prices of admission were increased during his stay. The last three days of his visit to Rouen, the General was publicly exhibited three times a day. From Rouen he proceeded to Amiens, where the same interest was excited by his diminutive size, and extraordinary facility of assuming and sustaining various characters. Thence he proceeded to Brussels, where all the seats in the theatre were taken eight days in advance. We understand that the watch, which was presented to the General by Queen Adelaide, and which was stolen from the table in the saloon during one of his exhibitions in Paris, has been recovered by the vigilance of the Paris police, and restored to him. At Brussels, however, a rush was made to the table, where his collection of valuable trinkets was placed during one of his exhibitions, and several, to the amount of 2,500 francs were carried off by the thieves. Fortunately, none of the presents bestowed on him by Queen Victoria, [King] Louis Phillipe, and the Duke of Devonshire, were among those thus lost (*Glasgow Courier* 17 July 1845)

All visitors to Brussels visit the field of the Battle of Waterloo, and Barnum and his followers were no different. They viewed the various well-known sites on the battlefield and were regaled with stories from Waterloo 'veterans', some of whom had probably never picked up a

La Butte du lion, the battle of Waterloo memorial in Belgium. Postcard

(Author's collection)

musket in their lives. Barnum, always on the lookout for interesting items for the American Museum, bought several mementos such as brass uniform buttons, cartridge cases, musket balls, and a three-inch piece of a leather boot recovered from the field.

Now that they were beginning to tour, exhibitions and performances had to be carefully planned and arranged before the company arrived in a town or city. Barnum now became the 'advance agent' for the shows and would arrive in a town several days before the planned arrival of the others in order to broker contracts with theatre managers, book hotels, and arrange printing and advertising. English was not always widely spoken, so this work was no mean feat for a man who spoke little French at the beginning. Often, he went to meetings with a large French – English dictionary tucked under his arm. Barnum's Copybook of letters that he wrote during 1845 – 1846 has survived and is a valuable source of information about the tour[7]. It also includes letters to the Editors of the *New York Atlas*, for whom he had offered himself as a foreign correspondent, reporting back on the culture, history, and daily life of the countries that he visited. These letters made an attractive travelogue for readers of the *Atlas*, as well as promoting his own interests as a 'well-travelled man'. Regarding his role as an advance agent, he writes;

> The usual duties of an avante-courier to an exhibition include amongst the most prominent that of raising an excitement by puffing the thing to be exhibited, and thus create with the public an appetite for seeing it. My duties are quite the reverse, my first business is to engage the largest Theatre or Saloon to be found in the town, then get out a simple placard announcing that the General will appear on such a day, after which all my energies are devoted to keeping the public <u>quiet</u>, and begging them <u>not to get excited</u> for we will endeavour to give them all a chance to see him – of course provided they 'down with the dust'. But ... they <u>will</u> get excited, and <u>will</u> keep talking about the marvellous little General ... The consequence is that when the General arrives we have a great deal of trouble in taking the money and finding places for all the people to get a look at him (Letter #69, 14 July 1845 in Tours)

Barnum was very clever at heightening the anticipation of the public for the arrival and subsequent exhibitions of Tom Thumb, although there appears to have been a lot more involved than the simple description that he gave above. A letter from Bordeaux gives an example;

> I have got the game all set right here, and have had 2000 small bills folded with one of General's cards placed in each & have had them delivered in the houses of all the rich families. I have also got 60 lithographs placed in the windows – posted 150 large bills – advertised in the papers – got the people d-d well excited and am

determined that the first four days they shall pay for all our trouble, for I have charged 3 francs for premier places & we will get it the first four days & can then reduce the price if we please (Letter #96, 22 August 1845 in Bordeaux)

Negotiations were always very fraught and often Barnum's first approach was to a local Mayor, who had the authority to accept or reject Barnum's proposals for both an exhibition and performance. Added to this were a complicated set of laws that Barnum always seemed at a loss to fully understand.

The laws in France about exhibitions are very funny. They are made to protect Theatres & in all the towns of France, except Paris, unless I can arrange with the manager of the theatre – he can by law take 15 per cent of my gross receipts & the Hospital can take 25 per cent of my gross receipts – in all 40 per cent! I have generally arranged with the managers to play in Theatre nights & get half gross receipts – saving to myself the privilege of playing day times without giving managers anything. And generally I have paid the Hospital from 5 to 20 Francs per day. But in Bordeaux I could not arrange. The manager claimed 15 per cent & the Hospice would not take less than 20 percent – in all 35 percent of my gross receipts. So I have given them a touch of Yankee[8] (Letter #93 26 August 1845 in Bordeaux)

The Hospital (or Hospice) tax that Barnum refers to was a form of 'poor tax' levied upon entertainments such as concerts and theatre performances. The *Commission des Hospices Civiles* in each town had the responsibility for raising funds for the relief of the poor and could set a tax rate on a case-by-case basis if they so wished. Much of Barnum's advance work was negotiating an agreeable rate with the Commissioners as well as negotiating terms with theatre managers. Saloons and other halls, as opposed to theatres, incurred no (or at least very little) charge on profits made. Wherever possible Barnum arranged for the General, as he now called him, to exhibit in these venues in the daytime and negotiated terms with theatre managers for evening performances of 'Tom Pouce', but things did not always go as he had planned;

> At Tours you play Petit Poucet [the drama]. The manager is a d-d rascal and I half fear he will have our bills taken down before you arrive for he did not want us to perform in the daytime. If so, you must get more printed. Unluckily the mayor refused me the hall in the Hotel Ville & as there was no other I was obliged to hire the Theatre from the d-d scamp which cost us including Bureaualists & Femme de Ports – 100 francs per day! – Curse him! (Letter #28, 9 August 1845 in Poitier)

And he was not afraid to lay the law down to intransigent and uncooperative theatre managers if necessary, as here when negotiations for the proposed visit to Bordeaux were stalling;

> I am much obliged for the promptness with which you answered my note of yesterday, and I very much request that your demands are such as to render it impossible for Genl Tom Pouce to visit Bordeaux. The General's expenses are very great … The General is a native of the United States of America. He comes a great distance with his family in order to gain an honest livelihood … The General is not exhibited simply as a <u>natural</u> curiosity, for as a natural curiosity alone, he would not receive 100 francs per day. But the chief attractions of his exhibitions are his performances., which consist of the Poses Academiques – dancing – singing – imitations of

celebrated characters, such as Grand Frederick etc. His exhibitions you will therefore perceive partake of the <u>dramatic</u>, and he is not therefore to be considered the same as a natural curiosity ... The General is an actor and a member of the Association des Artistes Dramatiques, as you will see by the book which accompanies this letter ... I will agree to pay you one quarter of the whole receipts of Tom Pouce in Bordeaux ... If you are willing to do this then I shall be most happy to make arrangements for him to visit this city – but if you persist in demanding a sum which he is wholly unable to pay then unfortunately ... he must return to Paris and England where the laws will permit him to gain a livelihood without taking from him all that he can earn. I sincerely hope that you will reconsider this matter, and consent to make an arrangement with me for it rests with you to decide whether he shall come to Bordeaux or not (Letter #52, 14 August 1845 in Saintes)

In this instance the manager refused to back down and Barnum was forced to find an alternative venue outside of the city limits and therefore free of any levies (see Letter #93 above).

Letter #28 above to Stratton Snr. goes on to give details of expenses and further instructions to the General's party;

Enclosed is list of expenses

The Theatre is Gratis – pay manager 0 per cent – nothing
Newspapers   <u>soft soap</u>!
Hospice (he claimed 10 per cent non 40 fr per day) for 3 days 60
Piano – don't know – Howard must arrange & get one
Printing 100 large and 1000 small bills   34.10

The printer has 2 cuts[9] – Don't forget them.

Price for Hotel is enclosed – breakfast at 8 or 9 o'clock or when you please in Coffee Room, you & Mrs S & Sherman – Dine at Table d'Hotel at 5 o'clock. Take the General whatever he likes to his room & pay accordingly.

Ponies as usual no agreement. The beds for domestics are 17 each – if Payne & Alfred sleep together I expect they save Francs but am not positive. ... PS Perhaps it will be a good dodge to have the equipage come upon the stage the first night, if not every night. It will set the people a talking. I've got them excited strong already.

What does become clear from the letters is the amount of work that Barnum was getting through in order for Tom Thumb to make an appearance, both in exhibition and in the stage drama. In most venues that they performed, a piano had to be hired and transported. Barnum was adept at advertising and arousing interest in the little General and

arranged for some of Tom Thumb's miniature clothing to be sent to him in advance of the party's arrival in a town so that it could be displayed. Several of the letters make requests to send items of clothing and boots as soon as possible—and not to forget to collect them when they left the town! It is also often forgotten that Tom Thumb's party consisted of up to 10 persons, and all had to be

Miniature boots belonging to Charles S Stratton (as General Tom Thumb). An American one cent coin gives an indication of scale (Barnum Museum, Bridgeport, Connecticut)

accommodated and fed, as detailed above. What is interesting to note from the letter is that the General appears to have dined alone in his room. Presumably, this was to keep him 'under wraps' and to avoid any unnecessary crowds when they dined.

Barnum wrote many letters a day, many of them to Stratton Snr. and Sherman, giving them instructions about where and when they should arrive, where they would be staying, and how he suggested General Tom Thumb to perform. Sometimes he would give performances of 'Tom Pouce' and at other times he would merely 'exhibit'. Performances changed according to the requirements of the particular venue;

> I could not arrange with the manager in the theatre except on condition that Genls performance should be different at night from the day. So they introduce him at night as Frederick the Great instead of Court Dress. Sherman must doctor up some kind of gammon to make the dress go off well. He had better come tattling in as Frederick the Great, with his cane in hand – take snuff etc – afterwards he can go on and talk about the King Louis Phillipe etc & same as in Court Dress. Then he can sing & when he gets ready to go off – coachy[10] must lead in the pony, Sherman must put the General on him and then he may ride off (Letter #44, 14 August 1845 in Saintes)

As an advance agent, Barnum was very much on his own. His days were long and involved many hours of travelling, sometimes by carriage, sometimes by rail, and even by river steamboat where available. The journey from Paris to Lille alone took 32 hours non-stop, except for a few minutes or so to change horses as necessary and a 15 minute 'comfort' stop to drink a cup of coffee and eat as much, and as quickly, as he could. Later in the tour Barnum would complain to 'Friend Roux' about the wrong information that he had been given regarding distances between towns and journey times. Roux had earlier written a piece for Tom Thumb entitled *Le Geant*. However, this was not a success and Barnum disliked Roux.

> ...you did not tell me right in regard the distances from town to town. For instance, you marked in my itinerary that the time to travel from Rennes to Brest was 8 hours – while in fact it was 27 hours. You marked from Geneva to Dijon 10 hours, but it would take us over 20 hours & past it. From Dijon to Strasbourg you marked 14 hours and as it is 310 kilometres will take 31 hours. From Strasbourg to Nancy is 21 hours – you marked 8 hours – in fact all the town range at least double the distance and time marked by you – which has deceived us exceedingly, caused us to lose much time and travel night and day to the injury of our healths (Letter #215, 10 October 1845 in Marseilles)

The constant travelling and wrangling with authorities were beginning to take their toll on Barnum's health. In the September he was in Toulouse and wrote to Hitchcock, his manager at the American Museum;

> I ought to be permitted to enjoy the fruits of my labour if I live, which I much fear will not be the case, as I am sadly afflicted with some painful and I fear fatal disease which appears seated at the pit of my stomach. I suffer much from it, and as I am on my legs during the whole day & generally travelling by diligence[11] through the whole night I am getting worse – I have lost all my fat – I am now fast losing my hair from the top of my head and if I don't lose my

life before I get home I shall be lucky (Letter #142, 12 September 1845 in Toulouse)

And he was homesick. He had not seen his wife and daughters since they returned to America sometime in June or July when he had begun his extensive French tour. Charity was suffering from an unspecified chronic illness, and she was now pregnant with their fourth child. He clearly missed them and was worried about them, especially his daughter Helen who was suffering from whooping-cough, a potentially deadly disease in children at this time. He had already lost one daughter to childhood illness. He despaired of her dying before he could return home.

> I am worn down with care and anxiety, continually kept on the rack
> by thoughts of all my affairs on both sides of the Atlantic, by fear
> of the death of my little Helen and by the most cursed annoyances
> incident to any man who tries to do business in France (Letter
> #219, 12 October 1845 in Marseilles)

Barnum was worn down with the balancing of his time and efforts in organising the tour, his concerns for his family, the affairs of his American Museum, and the acquisition of items for the Museum – and yet he was still driven to carry on, although by now he was becoming a little dispirited, and this comes across in the later letters from France. The tour continued unabated. In a letter to "Professor" Risley, a fellow performer, he gives a proposed itinerary;

> You ask where I am going and when I leave France. Here is my
> itinerary;

> Bordeaux 26th August to 9th September

Toulouse 13th to 20th September

Montpellier 24th to 28th September

Toulon, Avignon, Grenoble, Lyons 8th November to 27th

Geneva, Dijon, Strasbourg, Nancy, Metz, Liege, Brussels 29th December to 5th January [1846]

Antwerp, Ghent, Lille, Rouen, Haine 1st Feb to 6th Feb 1846

Caen, Amsterdam 13th to 22nd Feb

Hague, Rotterdam, Hamburg 27th March to 20th April

Berlin, Prague, Dresden, Leipzig, Vienna in May or June next year!

But I am not sure of going the whole route, for I am getting almost tired of travelling and beginning to feel that I have got money enough ... before going to America we must spend a few months in London, Scotland & Ireland for there is a good harvest there which we must reap if we live (Letter #62, 18 August 1845 Bordeaux)

In the letter he goes on to discuss the financial merits of going to St Petersburg and Vienna. By the time that he was in Marseilles, in October, he was writing that Russia and Austria held little temptation for him—and although he would have liked the extra money, he was feeling too homesick to go to those countries. He also had an invitation to take Tom Thumb to Italy but this he declined for the same reasons. However, while in Bordeaux he did accept an invitation to meet with Isabella, the Queen of Spain while the Royal Court was in Pamplona, Spain. Several of his letters in late August indicate that his intentions are to go to Pamplona but there is only one letter[12], dated September 12 from Pamplona to the Editors of the *Atlas*, that gives any mention of the actual visit made.

Around the time of their visit to Spain a strange notice appeared in the British press, a translation of a piece that appeared in the French newspapers. It first appeared in the *Morning Post* of the 8 September;

> A great sensation has been created at Nantes by the sudden disappearance of General Tom Thumb. The pygmy General wishing to attend the races at Quimper, left Vannes, with his suite at six o'clock, and was expected to have soon returned. Apartments had been previously engaged for him. His carriage broke down at Roasse ... inducing a very disagreeable delay. The postillion refused to wait the requisite time for the necessary repairs ... but he assured them that he would inform his master; and that another conductor should be immediately sent with fresh horses to continue their route. After waiting a considerable time the conductor and horses arrived, the repairs were completed, and General Tom Thumb mounted the carriage. Scarcely had they driven a league, than the horses stopped, the conductor descended, and perceived an immense heap of billets of wood; at the same instant four men, masked, seized and bound the driver, and threatened, if he uttered a cry, to shoot him. During this scene the General and his suite were locked in the arms of Morpheus. One of the four masks mounted the seat of the carriage and drove rapidly to St. Thurien. The carriage started to St. Thurien, to where is still unknown ... The most likely version is, that the four men in masks, belong to the band of Zino, called Comte d'Avenel, famed for his audacity and temerity. One fact is certain, that the General has not been seen or heard of since his departure.

This story was picked up by other national newspapers around the United Kingdom and continued to be printed for the next few days.

Some later accounts reported that he had been taken to Spain or that he was in Brittany. But was there any truth in the story? We know that Barnum was planning to take Tom Thumb and party to Pamplona in early September and he was certainly there when he wrote the letter to the editors of the *Atlas* on the 12 September. Of course, the reports in the British press could have been a mistranslation of a report in a French newspaper or even a piece of 'fake' news invented by a French editor and passed on to the British. Another possible explanation is that Barnum himself created the story. Knowing that he was planning to return to Britain at the end of 1845, he wanted to keep the interest in Tom Thumb alive in the minds of the British public. What better way than to create the story of a daring kidnap and then release it. It was on the 27th of September that news of the General's return appeared.

> By a private letter [from whom?], we learn that the General Tom Thumb is creating a great excitement at Toulouse; so that he appears to have been recovered from the brigands who carried him off, if, indeed, the adventure was not one of the marvels of the continental journals ... he will return to London about the end of January, when he will appear at one of the theatres in a fairy burlesque, written expressly for him by Mr Albert Smith (*Illustrated London News* 27 September 1845)

Interestingly, nobody in the General's party makes any reference to this supposed episode and Barnum himself makes only two fleeting references to it in his Copybook;

> I hope my letter of yesterday calms your fears about the safety of the General. We never heard of the Bandits till we received your letter (Letter #111, 3 September 1845 in Bordeaux)

> You perceive that we are yet in the land of the living, notwithstanding
> the late reports of the Generals being taken into Spanish captivity
> by the Brigands (Letter #440, 5 December 1845 London)

If the reports of the kidnap had been true, then I feel certain that Barnum would have capitalised on them and milked all the publicity from them that he could. The incident might possibly also have featured as part of Tom Thumb's exhibition.

Barnum's visit to Europe had several purposes. He wanted to make money; to promote his protégé, General Tom Thumb; to promote his American Museum and his self-interests; and to gather interesting items for the museum. The tour certainly generated a lot of money and raised Barnum's status. It also gathered a lot of exhibition material that was shipped back to the United States of America. Barnum had a ready eye for the unusual and interesting. He and his colleagues bought a vast quantity of paintings, engravings, ceramics, Roman antiquities, panoramas and dioramas, optical and scientific instruments, unusual shells, and even exotic bird skins, as detailed in Letter #472, 22 December 1845. Most of these were destined for the museum but some items did end up in Barnum's own home.

> I have bought a set of mechanical trumpets for $500 which
> will take place of my Band – be ten times better and save their
> cost in 6 months   I have also engaged an anatomical venus – for
> a separate room in my museum – also a moving panorama &
> diorama representing the Funeral of Napoleon   I also bought in
> London   a Physioscope (optical instrument) and 3 or 4 slides for
> my Dissolving views. As these are scientific works and are for an
> Institution Publique (museum) I believe, hope, and trust there is

no duty on them. The cost of the whole was £29.10 (Letter#352, 11 November 1845 in Paris)

It was not only physical objects that Barnum was interested in, he was also eager to obtain natural (human) curiosities. While in Bordeaux he came across a 'giant' whom he wished to engage for the museum, but he must have demanded terms that Barnum found unacceptable;

> The Giant must suppose that golden Napoleons[13] grow upon trees in America, to ask such a price for going there. In the first place he does not need but one person to travel with him, nor even that unless it is his wife. Here is my last and best offer. I will advance 1000 francs to pay his expenses to New York. Besides which sum I will pay him 9000 francs for exhibiting six months in America according to the directions of my agent and in such places as my agent shall select ... I reserving to myself the privilege of renewing the engagement for six months longer by paying him 10,000 francs more for the second six months (Letter #98, 27 August in Bordeaux)

He came across another potential human exhibit, albeit somewhat disturbing by today's standards, while in Paris. He wrote to Hitchcock, the manager at the museum;

> I have seen twice within the last week the most stupendous curiosity which God ever permitted to exist and which will make our fortunes in double quick time if I can get it into the museum ... It is a living child with two heads! It is now three months old and it is perfectly healthy ... it would draw a cart load of silver every week. I have offered the parents 60 dollars per month for 1st year - $100 per month for 2nd year, $150 per month for 3rd, $200 per month

for 4th, $250 per month for 5th and 400 per month for 1 or 10 years following besides I pay wages & expenses of parents. They laugh at the offer (although they are poor) and say they will not at present make me any offer. But I am going at them again. Now suppose I gave $100 per week & all expenses for one year – could we afford that for the museum? Could we offer more? ... It does not strike me as an offensive sight ... Guilladeau[14] will of course say – touch it not – for it is a monstrosity, but we care not for that, we go for dollarstrosity (Letter #350, 10 November 1845 in Paris)

If any letter in the collection underlines Barnum's attitude towards making money, then I think this one does. For all that his letters to his wife and daughter show the caring human side of the man, there are times, such as in the above, where he also shows himself to lack empathy and humanity. Human curiosities were merely commodities that could be bought and exhibited for profit. His opening sentence shows this, as his first thought appears to be that money could be made quickly from the unfortunate child. Money is a frequent theme of many of his letters. Often, he complains at the amount of money he has to lay out at each venue (mainly to theatre managers and Hospice Commissioners). In Letter #20, to his friend Risley, he intimates that he might have considered ending the tour when he had made $50,000 but that he was not yet satisfied until they had made an anticipated $100,000. Several of his letters are concerned with the financial affairs of the American Museum. Letter #219 to Hitchcock expresses his hopes that the museum will make a $20,000 profit for the year. Even in a letter to his wife he discusses the museum's finances;

He has given me the returns of the last quarter at the museum which shows the profit to have been $3361 after paying rent and all other expenses – this is at the rate of $13444.00 per year, and it is better than the museum ever did before (the same three months) except last year when we had the Giants (Letter #83, 25 August 1845 in Bordeaux)

So financial matters were never far from his mind. There is an argument to be made that Barnum was driven by the acquisition of money and status. It has to be agreed that much of his money he did invest into expanding his museum empire but some of his wealth was also expressed in the property that he had built in Bridgeport. Although it would not be built until he returned to America, he did outline his ideas to his wife in Letter #37;

I hope you will be able to make good arrangements about our new house in Bridgeport. I do not want it exactly like any other ... I want plenty of trees about the house – not too many – with two large gates in front for a carriage to enter one, and making a turn of a half moon like this go out at the other [here he makes a rough sketch]. I want a nice smooth lawn to extend around the whole house – then at a little distance back I want a flower and fruit garden & hot house, then clear at the back of that I want the vegetable garden. If convenient I would like a fishpond not far off, but I am not particular about that, as I can arrange that afterwards. I want another entrance leading to the lawn & carriage house which mist stand at some distance away from the house ... you had better not decide positively on buying a place till I have learned all the particulars of price, the quantity of land &c (Letter #37, 13 August 1845 in Rochefort)

Even in laying his dreams before his wife—money was still in his thoughts. And it was money, or the tailing off of the tour profits, that precipitated an earlier close and return to England than had at first been planned. By the time that Barnum had reached Bordeaux, he was homesick, lonely, and feeling ill. The acrimonious negotiations that he had had with the theatre manager and the Hospice Commissioners had taken their toll and he was becoming dispirited. He was developing a very jaundiced view of the French, something that was reflected in a letter to Stratton Snr.

> It is very certain that we can make much more money in England than we can in France, and we can make it ten times easier, for it is too hard for any live man to travel and do business in this Frenchified lying thieveing [sic] robbing swindling country. I never had so much hard work and trouble before in my life as I have every day with the thieveing [sic] rascals, and after all I can do they will lie and cheat you out of what little you can take ... I would not stay here in France much longer to save them all from hell and I am satisfied that we had better travel right ahead and get out of the country and lose a few days in order to do so ... we will soon make up our lost time after we get to England (Letter #212, 3 October 1845 in Marseilles)

He goes on to propose that the tour go to Toulon, Lyon and then on to Paris for a second time until December 1 and that they move on to Haine and sail for England on December 6. Barnum himself would return to London for a short stay in mid-October to arrange performances in the city on the General's return at the end of the year. He then returned to Paris to arrange the final exhibitions before closing the continental tour.

While in Paris in November, Barnum, the General, and their entourage met with the King of France for a third and final time.

He gave his various performances and before leaving he was literally loaded with presents, each person rushing to give him a keepsake. He received presents from the King, Queen, Comte de Paris, Princess Adelaide, Duchess de Orleans &c. They consisted of diamond pins & rings, gold chains, elegant boxes and caskets inlaid with pearl & precious stones, souvenirs &c &c (Letter #406, 29 November 1845 in Paris)

Barnum was also to receive a purse of 500 francs after this meeting with the French Royalty.

All eyes were now set for a (hopefully) triumphant return to London. The tour of France, Brussels, and Pamplona had been long and arduous. Barnum had expressed how much the tour had affected him but there is no record of how General Tom Thumb, his parents, nor other members of the travelling group felt about the tour. The little General had been exhibited throughout the country, regularly performing twice a day—and sometimes three times—at whatever town they happened to be in. And it has to be remembered that this was a child no older than nine years at the most. But Barnum still had plans for him. He had been performing in the dramatic piece entitled Petit Poucet but, with a view to a London return, Barnum had wanted to expand it into a piece that would be known in English as *Hop o'my Thumb*. He wrote to the dramatist Albert Smith;

We have concluded to have you go ahead and revamp 'Petit Poucet' making such additions & alterations as your judgement shall dictate. You propose to entirely reconstruct the piece with good burlesque dialogue all in verse and jokes for £50 – or to do it in simple prose for £25. Now my dear fellow, I don't know which will take the best, the poetry or prose, and therefore leave it entirely to

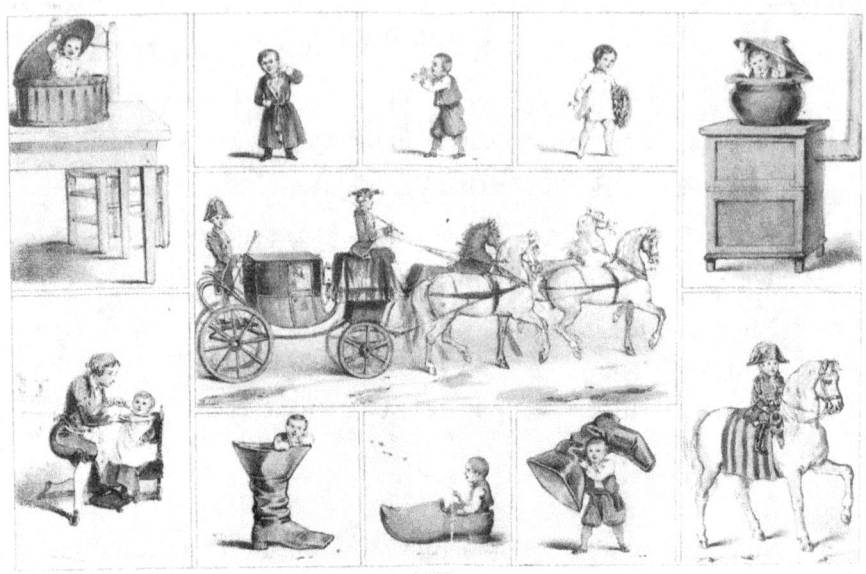

Scenes from the drama Tom Pouce at the Théatre du Vaudeville Paris 1845 (BnF Paris)

you – we want the best thing that can be turned out, and if it will be better in poetry than prose, we prefer to have the former & pay you £50. We want something wonderfully 'steep' – particularly stunning – something overrunning with jokes & cream that will take in any country and if you stick in several comic duets or trios, the General and his little coachy & footman can sing them. I asked the General what I should request you to add to the piece – he says he wants you to add the old English catch – 'Three blind mice' – for him, his coachy & footman to sing.

One great fault of Petit Poucet is as you say, the five acts – 2 or 3 are sufficient; another fault is, there is not half enough for the General to do … he can do anything that any actor can do … and he can come the pantomime to any extent & talk as much as you please. If you choose to introduce the statues do so, though perhaps you can introduce other things which will be better. You can introduce him in a muff, or small work basket, or beer pot, or as many other things as you please – he can strut the dandy – or meditate as Napoleon – and as many other dodges as you desire (Letter #165, 19 September 1845 in Toulouse)

And so, Barnum's tour of France came to a close in early December and it was announced in the British press that General Tom Thumb had made his return;

General Tom Thumb has returned to England, laden with honours and presents; and announces some farewell levees at his old quarters, in the Egyptian Hall. The little hero has become a perfect Frenchman in his absence, and is reported, if anything, to have diminished in size: at all events, he is not an inch taller, and has never had the least indisposition (*Illustrated London News* 13 December 1845)

The stage was now set for the next chapter in Barnum's European visit.

Notes

1   A peaked cotton cap.

2   Fanny Ellsler was a famous, and beautiful, Austrian born ballet dancer of the period.

3   *Sun (London)* 24 March 1845.

4   *Western Times* 3 May 1845.

5   *Lancaster Gazette* 3 May 1845.

6   Stratton, as Tom Thumb, was now performing in a stage version of the fairy story of 'Tom Thumb', or 'Tom Pouce' in French, in which he played the hero.

7   *P. T. Barnum Letter Copybook 1845-1846* The Barnum Museum. Online at; https://collections.ctcdigitalarchive.org

8   To avoid paying unnecessary costs, Barnum discovered a saloon in a park outside of the city limits and arranged to perform there. The municipality of Bordeaux had no jurisdiction outside of the city limits.

9   Woodcuts of images for the printer.

10 Coachman.

11 A form of carriage.

12 Letter #476.

13 A French gold coin.

14 Emile Guilladeau was the Director of Natural History exhibits at Barnum's American Museum.

CHAPTER 6 – ENGLAND REVISITED

Towards the end of October 1845, Barnum paid a brief visit to London to prepare the way for what he hoped would be the triumphant return of General Tom Thumb. Much of his time was spent in contacting theatre managers in the hope of securing a venue for his performances. On October 27 he wrote to Mr Webster, the manager of the Adelphi theatre;

> A simple translation of his French play of Petit Poucet played 63 consecutive nights at the Vaudeville Theatre Paris would be nearly all that would be required ... The accessories weighing a couple of tons are now in Lyons. We carry them from town to town in a vehicle expressly devoted to it. Among the rest is his little palace and furniture, all including the candelabra being of the most gorgeous description ... The General performs several characters in the piece – among which is Frederick the Great in which he mounts his own pony and goes in pursuit of the ogre. He also appears in a pie – in the Giants boot which he draws from the Giants foot while asleep – in a soup pot on the stove &c &c His little equipage also appears in the play (carriage drawn by 4 ponies) ... here is much acting by the General, and he cannot be beat by old or young great or small in pantomime or anything else appertaining to the business (Letter #277, 27 October 1845)

But Barnum's powers of persuasion were not to work in this instance. Stratton did not appear at the Adelphi Theatre but was engaged at the Theatre Royal Lyceum for March and April 1846, under the management of Mrs Keeley. He appeared in *Hop o' my Thumb*, the burlesque piece written for him by Albert Smith. It is true that a "Tom Thumb" did appear at the Adelphi but this was to be shown as an imitator, of which there would be many. A report in the press qualifies this after a man named Hannan was charged with the attempted murder of his wife in Drury-lane, London.

> The accused [Hannan] by the accounts in some papers, is said to
> be the father of General Tom Thumb. To avoid mistake, we beg to
> state that it is not the renowned general, but a youth who has been
> playing at the Adelphi Theatre under that name (*Morning Herald
> (London)* 19 June 1846)

Stratton, as General Tom Thumb, did finally make his appearance at the Adelphi theatre in December of 1846, a year after his return to England, where he appeared in *Hop o' my Thumb*[1].

Failing to confirm an engagement at a London theatre for December 1845, Barnum negotiated with the managers of the Egyptian Hall for an exhibition space. He made it clear that he would only rent the Hall if certain conditions were met. On his return to Paris at the end of October he wrote to Mr Clarke at the Egyptian Hall;

> Can I have the front room that time & if so at what rent
> Will she (Mrs Lackington) have the light from the roof arranged
> and put the back room in good order, and if so what rent for that
> a month

... One thing is very certain viz; no respectable exhibition will ever open in that back room upstairs until it is renovated decorated and put in order. If I owned the Egyptian Hall I would not allow that room to be seen till it was properly arranged, for its appearance is an injury to the character of the Hall. I have several fine exhibitions in France, which I hope to exhibit in Egyptian Hall before shipping them to America, but too much pains cannot be taken to have the saloons appear neat & respectable (Letter #288, 31 October 1845)

It would seem that these demands were met, and that the Hall was engaged because back in London in early December he wrote to Stratton Snr. confirming that he had engaged the Egyptian Hall for two weeks commencing the 15th of December. After this time, the group would be moving on to Newcastle upon Tyne and then on to Edinburgh for the New Year. He was also negotiating with William Batty, the manager of Astley's Amphitheatre in London for a short run there[2].

Barnum was hoping for an immediately successful return to London, and although he may have engaged the Egyptian Hall for a short period, the feelings in his December letters display a disappointment. In a letter to Albert Smith about the new performance piece for the General he writes;

My present opinion is that the General will not play in London for the present and therefore we can give you more time to finish his piece. Since hearing the first act yesterday, I quite fear that it may have one fault (and I fear only one) viz; brevity. I more than half think you had better make 8 acts of it. I fear it would not do for us to talk to a manager about playing our new piece – unless that new piece took an hour or more for its performance (Letter #442, 5 December 1845)

And in a subsequent letter to Stratton Snr. the following day, he outlines some of the difficulties facing them;

> Things still look very dull in England. I have had a long interview with Titus [a showman friend of Barnum] advertiser to find that we have been already to all the principal good towns in this country. We can't go to Oxford and Cambridge till February on account of the vacations – we can't go to Scotland till March on account of snow & how we shall make out in dodging about the best towns we can find in England is a matter of uncertainty. I wish to the God that we were safely in America – however we may find on trying that our business here will be better than prospects indicate. It seems almost necessary to open here one week merely to get time to start ... I am going to try the Adelaide Gallery[3] today, for if they stand all expenses & give us half & if besides we can get a few nights at the uptown theatres, it will not be bad (Letter #445, 6 December 1845)

Despite the problems facing the forthcoming exhibition and subsequent tour, Barnum was the eternal optimist. He was soon embarking on his advertising campaign with enthusiasm. Mobile advertising vans appear to have been one of his major schemes for promoting the exhibition.

> I can probably have some of the vans on Monday next which are now used by the Cattle Show. At all events I shall have similar vans, with both ends covered, the driver going on foot – and in that case I think therefore you had better print a large bill for one end of the van ... On the other end we will put the smaller bills and Cuts size of life. You may print 100 of those large ones for the end of the vans for I can use the balance of them in the country. I think that you

had better add the following to the mammoth bill for the side of the vans – 'Admission 1 shilling – Children under 12 years half price' … I shall expect to get out my boardmen early Wednesday morning. (Letter #456, 8 December 1845)

Barnum also arranged for a band to play every morning outside of the Egyptian Hall to draw attention to the exhibition. It is interesting to note that he is now offering a half price admission for children, whereas in his previous exhibitions of 1844 there had been a flat rate admission price of 1 shilling.

The British press heralded the return of General Tom Thumb in several national newspapers;

GENERAL TOM THUMB will arrive from Paris, and commence his EXHIBITION at the EGYPTIAN HALL, Piccadilly, on MONDAY NEXT, the 15th inst., for Twelve Days only, being his Farewell Appearance in London, previous to his final departure for America. He will be in Newcastle Dec. 29 and 30, and in Edinburgh, New Year's-day and week (*Morning Herald (London)* 11 December 1845)

Although Barnum made sure that announcements of his forthcoming exhibition at the Egyptian Hall were made nationally, there was very little subsequent press coverage of the exhibition itself. One of the few comments on the response to the exhibition was made in the *London Evening Standard* of 27 December, where it referred to the visitors who 'flocked about him pretty plentifully, as they are apt to do whenever he is within reach.' The same piece also referred to how the little General's performances 'elicited the customary marks of wonderment'. There is a sense that Stratton was not creating the stir that he did when he first arrived in London in 1844. And little wonder, because at the Egyptian Hall while he was exhibiting there were other attractions. The Mammoth Horse, named 'General Washington', was on display. This was owned by Carter, the 'Lion King', and stood around 21 hands[4] high at the shoulder and weighed 3,000 pounds. Also on display in the building were two models by Captain Siborne of the Battle of Waterloo; the Napoleon Museum with relics in connection with the French Emperor; and two pygmy African children known as "The Boshiemen Children". In fact, and I am sure much to Barnum's chagrin, there were now several rivals to Charles Stratton. *The Leamington Spa Courier* of 27 December 1845 informed that;

> THE GERMAN DWARFS - An advertising notice informs us that, on Monday next, we are to be astonished by the sight of *three* dwarfs of the same family, whose mimic representations have won the smiles of Royalty, and the applause of crowded audiences, both in the metropolis and elsewhere. We suppose that we should be insulting the taste of some, if we were not to anticipate their attendance at the approaching exhibition.

Queen Victoria records that these German dwarfs were also presented at Buckingham Palace before they were put on public display.

> After dinner we saw 3 German dwarfs, aged 22, 18, & 13. The girl of 18 is a pretty, healthy looking young woman, but the boys are very frightful, between the height of Bertie & Alice (*Queen Victoria's Journal Vol 18 P203* 16 December 1845)

On the same day as the *Leamington Spa Courier* report, the *Illustrated London News* carried this item;

The three German dwarfs (The Pictorial Times *15 June 1845)*

THE MINIATURE JOHN BULL – A companion, or, in some respects, rival to 'General Tom Thumb', has just appeared at the Exhibition Rooms of the Society of British Artists, in Pall Mall East. He was born at Kittesford, near Taunton, Somerset; his age is 16 years; height, 34 inches. He is of symmetrical proportions and is really a very ingenious dwarf. He performs an entertainment in six scenes – John Bull; the British Sailor; Napoleon; Shaw, the Life Guardsman; a Poacher; and the 'Old English Gentleman … The performance is, we assure our readers, very interesting; and, as one of the miniature world, he will prove one of the holiday sights of the ensuing week.

If that was not enough, across at the Drury Lane theatre a Miss Turner was appearing as the character Tom Thumb in a pantomime based on Gulliver's Travels. London appeared to have been awash with dwarf performers, and Stratton did not command the novelty factor that he once had—at least not in the metropolis. It was time for Barnum to make a return to the provinces and head north to Newcastle.

It was a cold two-day sojourn in the city but, as always, Barnum's mind was on business matters. In a letter to Moses Kimble in New York he wrote;

> General & Co are all well. We go to Edinburgh tomorrow, make the tour of Scotland & Ireland, then give them one more farewell twist in England & sail for home sometime between March & July. We took £230 in London the last 2 days & many persons went away unable to get in   I have been talking seriously with the present proprietor of the Chinese Collection in London about bringing it to America – but find it would cost too much. Can't you get for you, or me or both of us, some Captain or Steward of a ship sailing to China, to buy a lot of Chinese Curiosities & bring them over at a fair price. I would like much to have say $3000 worth, taking the most striking subjects that could be selected for the Collection now in Boston (Letter #495, 30 December 1845)

By the turn of the year, Barnum and company found themselves in Edinburgh but not before stopping off for one day for a performance in Leith[5]. His letter of January 1 to his wife[6] is long and rambling, and it is clear that he longs to be back home in America. He considers taking a passage early but has decided against it because of the inclement Atlantic weather. He is harassed with the tour, his museum business— as he had bought the Peale Museum and also now had an interest in the Baltimore Museum—and thoughts of home. Another problem that has arisen for him is closing the tour early and returning to America in February. Stratton's parents say that if they go then they expect to have the whole of the profits. This is something that Barnum feels does not justly belong to them. There is a feeling that his hand is being forced and that the tour should continue. As he explained to his wife, the plan was to make a brief tour of Scotland, a quick visit to Ireland and then back to London, after which time he would then return to America—and be satisfied. He later modified his plans to return to London on 1 March, stay for three months, then a quick provincial tour of England, and then back to America. However, the Strattons appear to have become more forceful in their dealings with Barnum. He had been putting together a book concerning the 'Travels of Tom Thumb' but some of the content infuriated Stratton Snr. In a letter to his colleague Brettell Barnum explains;

> I enclose you the book corrected & amended. Mr Stratton has just discovered that in it I am called the guardian of Genl Tom Thumb, and he says – 'By God it shall be took out, or my boy shall never sell a damned book – you might as well say he has got no father and done with it' Now if it should be said that he had no father, or at least not much of one, it would not be far out of the way. But I pray you, sink the 'Guardian' for truth to tell the father needs one much more than the son (Letter #528, 5 January 1846)

One assumes that this was done and that Stratton Snr. was appeased, as no further mention is made of the matter. The incident does call into question how Barnum perceived his relationship with Charles Stratton. The boy was a means of making money for Barnum and therefore a commodity. Throughout his records, Barnum often refers to being the 'agent', 'proprietor', 'secretary', or 'manager' of General Tom Thumb. These are all business terms, but the use of the word 'guardian' takes on a different note. It implies a more formal legal relationship, in which the guardian takes on a familial responsibility for the minor. It is understandable how Stratton Snr. could become offended by this, as he was present throughout the whole tour as Charles Stratton's father; he had not abdicated his paternal responsibility to Barnum.

Barnum's arrival in Edinburgh did not immediately draw the crowds that he had anticipated, given the response in 1844. The press noted that;

> He is not attracting such vast crowds as flocked around him on his previous visit, but the visitors are still numerous, and he is still as lively and entertaining as ever (*Fife Herald* 6 January 1846)

The Scottish tour continued. From Edinburgh it moved to Glasgow and then on to the provincial towns of Kircaldy, St Andrews, Dunfermline, Fife, Perth, Cupar, Dundee, and as far north as Aberdeen, amongst others. In order to maximise profits, Barnum advertised a reduced performance charge;

> Admission 1s Children under ten, half price. In order to accommodate the WORKING CLASS. A FOURTH LEVEE (including ALL his performances) will commence at a quarter before Nine o'clock – the admission to which will be REDUCED to each person (*Dundee, Perth & Cupar Advertiser* 23 January 1846)

This presumably was quite a successful move as it continued throughout the Scottish tour and beyond, making General Tom Thumb's performances accessible to all levels of society. It is possible that the increased crowds drawn by this reduced admission scheme may have contributed to the accident that occurred in Airdrie during one of the performances.

> NARROW ESCAPE OF TOM THUMB – The floor of the Town-hall at Airdrie, where General Tom Thumb was exhibiting at a cheaper rate to the working classes, on Monday evening, gave way from the pressure, and precipitated three hundred people into a smith's shop below. Fortunately, no one was killed, though one man had his leg broken. The table on which the General had been performing a few minutes before the accident fell with the mass, and was crushed to pieces (*Kentish Gazette* 3 March 1846)

Barnum makes little reference to this incident and only initially in a brief letter to a Mr Smith;

> The floor broke through at Airdrie – one arm and one leg broke and 39 more injured. It will cost us a few hundred pounds probably. It was not at the Court House – but at the Theatre which I engaged for the 6d fellows [the working class]. None of us were hurt. We have done miserable business lately;
>
> Airdrie - £31
> Greenoch - £20 ditto £41
> Paisley - £23
> Glasgow £30
> (Letter #598, 19 February 1846)

Once again, it appears that his concern for monetary matters outweighs any concern for the victims of the accident. However, he did later write to the town authorities with a donation of twenty pounds on behalf of General Tom Thumb, to be distributed amongst the poorest persons who suffered in the accident. But this was only after he had been approached by two representatives from Airdrie, presumably solicitors, asking whether the General would be inclined to make a donation towards the victims. A later letter implied that both the General and Barnum had been threatened with litigation over the matter, but that it was out of charity that the donation had been sent. There was also an accusation that Barnum had been informed that the floor was weak and would only hold a few hundred people and that there was a clear danger that it might collapse. Barnum refuted these accusations as a tissue of ridiculous lies;

> The truth was we were informed in advance by the proprietor that the hall had held 1000 persons at a time, and could do so again, and it was repeatedly stated to him that our object in getting the hall was to get in more people than the other hall could possibly hold and that we wished the people to be packed as thick as they could stand ... We were constantly urging the audience to approach the table where the General was exhibiting, to get as near him as they could. Should we have encouraged this extra weight to concentrate about him had we ever received the [-] hint that the floor would not have sustained as many as could have stood on it? (Letter #607, 24 February 1846)

The letter goes on to make it clear that if the authorities should be unwilling to accept Barnum's perceived facts in the matter, that General Tom Thumb would be prepared to take legal advice to counter any claim made upon him. Unfortunately, we do not have copies of letters sent to Barnum so there is no record of the response to the above letter. In fact, Barnum does not raise the matter again in any official capacity, other than recounting the incident in general.

If the General had had a lucky escape in Airdrie, there was a potentially more dangerous incident earlier in Glasgow. In January, while he and Sherman were making their way to the Kings Arms Inn they were surrounded by a group of youths. At first, they thought that they were there to welcome the General to Glasgow, but it soon became clear that their intentions were otherwise. They jostled and prodded the pair quite offensively and, in an act of desperation, Sherman lashed out with his foot and kicked one of the boys in the groin. The boy was carried home in pain and a complaint was lodged against Sherman for the assault. He was arrested and taken before the local magistrate. The evidence was heard on both sides and Sherman was fined two guineas. The General, although shaken by the events, was unharmed.

Another sad occurrence took place in mid-January. One of the miniature horses that pulled Stratton's carriage suddenly died in transit by rail on the way to Glasgow. Stratton was very upset at this as it had been his favourite pony, but Barnum was never one to miss an opportunity. The hide was removed from the carcass and sent to a naturalist in Glasgow for preservation. It was then shipped to Barnum's American Museum where M. Guilladeau would work his taxidermy skills to have the pony mounted for display.

Although Barnum had stated his intentions of making a visit to Ireland, there appears to be little record of this. He did mount at least one exhibition there because it was recorded that at the end of February Stratton, as General Tom Thumb, performed before the inmates of the

*The English dwarf (*The Pictorial Times *3 January 1846)*

Belfast Lunatic Asylum[7]. The performance was apparently well received, but one might expect any performance in such an institution would be. Barnum himself wrote no letters from Ireland, nor does he refer to the visit. Clearly, Barnum appears to have been unable to secure engagements for Stratton in Ireland. This may have reflected an apathy in Ireland towards the Tom Thumb character or, as seems more likely, Barnum was eager to return to London where he felt more money could be made. I consider that it was also highly likely that he wanted to be back in London to counter the swell of interest in another immitation act—the 'English Tom Thumb' or 'Field-Marshall Tom Thumb' as he was also known, in a calculated attempt to 'pull rank' on the General. This character appears to have filled the vacuum left by Barnum's General Tom Thumb during the provincial tour and, having initially exhibited in the Exhibition Rooms of the Society of British Artists, had now moved to the Egyptian Hall. Barnum may have feared that the 'impostor' exhibiting at the Egyptian Hall might have an effect on his own protégé. In fact, in January the 'English Tom Thumb' issued a challenge to General Tom Thumb;

CHALLENGE to the AMERICAN DWARF, GENERAL TOM THUMB – The English Dwarf, Field Marshal TOM THUMB, now exhibiting daily at the Egyptian Hall, Piccadilly, ... challenges to the field his American rival, who has assumed the title of Tom Thumb (a name long known in British history), to appear and perform with him in public, so that their respective admirers may judge of their comparative merits (*Lloyd's Weekly Newspaper* 25 January 1846)

It is surprising that Barnum did not take up this challenge as it would have made for some excellent publicity—a General versus a Field Marshal with the prospect of 'Dwarf Wars'. But he seems to have completely ignored it. So much so that in February, another piece appeared in the press, lauding the exploits of 'Field Marshal Tom Thumb' and pointing out that he was still awaiting a response from Barnum and General Tom Thumb. The impostor was certainly emulating the General;

Field Marshal Tom Thumb, the English Dwarf, who has lately created such a sensation, and who is daily performing at the Egyptian Hall, Piccadilly, appeared on Monday evening at the Pavilion Theatre in a new one-act farce, entitled 'Tom Thumb at Home'. The piece was written for the express purpose of testing his dramatic powers, and they are most extraordinary ... He has innumerable provincial engagements and is only now awaiting the arrival of the American dwarf General Tom Thumb, whom he has challenged to appear and perform with him in public (*Shipping and Mercantile Gazette* 14 February 1846)

The challenge not being accepted, Barnum returned to London in early March, via Oxford. Here, Stratton was presented with an Oxonian academic Gown and Cap. General Tom Thumb began a series of performances in *Hop o'my Thumb* by Albert Smith at the Lyceum Theatre and from the 9th of March he also began exhibiting at the Egyptian Hall, the impostor Tom Thumb making some performances at Astley's Amphitheatre before setting out on his own provincial tour. Two Tom Thumbs in London at the same time drew a withering response from Barnum;

NO DECEPTION – INFAMOUS FALSEHOOD A shameful attempt has been for some time, and is now making, to disparage the merits of the English dwarf FIELD-MARSHAL TOM THUMB, who is announced by Mr Widdicomb and Mr Carter, the 'Lion King', to appear at ASTLEY'S AMPHITHEATRE on the MAMMOTH HORSE, on Monday next, March 16, on the occasion of Mr Widdicomb's Benefit. The American dwarf (to quote his bills), is stated to be 25 inches high, and Mr Barnum, his proprietor, now asserts that the English dwarf is four times that height, consequently the Field-Marshal must be a perfect giant … The public will judge for themselves (*Morning Advertiser* 13 March 1846)

Hop o'my Thumb continued to play at the Lyceum Theatre throughout March, and Barnum also managed to secure one-night engagements at the City of London Theatre and the Royal Marylebone Theatre. Again, it was an intensive period for Stratton as he was exhibiting at the Egyptian Hall in the afternoons and early evenings before moving to the theatres to perform at night—and remember that in reality Stratton was only in his ninth year! Albert Smith had managed to condense the lengthy fairy story into a series of short scenes and the piece was written in a burlesque style. For anyone who is specifically interested in Smith's adaptation, the *Illustrated London News*[8] gave a lengthy scene by scene description of the plot which aptly demonstrates how Stratton's miniscule stature fits into the story.

Barnum arranged a re-engagement of the General for the Lyceum Theatre during April that would continue through to the end of May, with occasional performances at both the City of London Theatre and St James' Theatre. Business was good at last. In Letter #717 to his wife, dated 2 April 1846, he tells her that the three performances at the Egyptian Hall are making $500 daily and the evening performances at the Lyceum are making $200 daily. He must have then entrusted management of the performances to Stratton Snr. and Sherman because in mid-April he made a return visit to America. This was to catch up with his museum business, as there had been suggestions that he might want to sell, something that Barnum clearly was against;

> I will however state one simple fact, which will show the folly of my selling even so far as interest is concerned, which is but a small objection compared to that of having others concerned in the direction of the museum.
>
> I gave for the American Museum $12,000
>
> If I should demand $50,000 it, it would be looked on as an exorbitant demand – but if a person should give me $100,000 cash for it and I took that cash and put it out to interest at 7 per cent it would yield me - $7000, whereas the museum now yields me easily & without risque $15,000 - $18,000 – and I feel certain of making it pay a nett profit of £25,000 to $30,000 per annum before I am three years older. If a man should tomorrow offer me $150,000 cash down for the American Museum and at the same time bind me not

to engage in similar business in America, I should certainly decline the offer (Letter #641, 18 March 1846)

Barnum had another important reason for returning to America at this time;

> Mr P T Barnum, the American gentleman who brought Tom Thumb to England ... sails this morning in the *Great Western* for New York. Mr Barnum, who has a keen eye for the extraordinary in nature, takes out with him a fine living chimpanzee, or African ourang outang [sic], which he recently purchased for six hundred guineas, from the proprietors of the Surrey Zoological Gardens ... Mr Barnum has purchased the chimpanzee for his American Museum, New York, and also for the Baltimore museum, of which he has recently become the proprietor ... Mr Barnum's spirit in procuring the creature at such a heavy outlay for the gratification of his countrymen is really deserving of praise (*Caledonian Mercury* 13 April 1846)

In the passenger list for that voyage, Mrs Stratton was also listed. At the end of March, he had written requesting two berths on the ship, one of which should be for Mrs Stratton who was going to America 'on a visit'[9]. The second berth was stated to have been for her brother but then Barnum makes the revelation that *he* is the second passenger and that he wishes the fact to be kept a secret as he wanted to surprise his family and friends in America. There is no mention of her or Barnum's return, although later newspaper reports of the final departure of General Tom Thumb make mention of them. In a letter to General Tom Thumb, sent from Bridgeport[10], Barnum explains that his wife continues to be unwell but that he might set out to England on 1 June but if not, he would certainly leave on 16 June to be back for 30 June.

The Highland dwarfs (Illustrated London News *30 May 1846*)

While General Tom Thumb's chief rival, The English Tom Thumb or 'Field Marshal' as he called himself, was now on a provincial tour, the public appetite for all things miniature still abounded. Next to make an appearance in the metropolis were the Highland Dwarfs. Under the management of Mr Mackenzie, these three siblings—two boys and a girl —were to make an exhibition at the Cosmorama Rooms on Regent-street three times a day from mid-May[11]. They presented the Highland sword dance and other Scottish dances as well as the boys exhibiting the broadsword drill. Royal patronage swelled audience numbers, as they had been presented to the Queen at Buckingham Palace.

I then saw, with my 3 (the D^{ss} being there) 3 Highland Dwarfs, who though certainly not pretty are very extraordinary. They are 2 brothers & a sister, aged 22, 19, & 18 very strongly built. They danced and sang (*Queen Victoria's Journal Vol 21 P185* 15 May 1846)

Queen Victoria clearly had a fascination with dwarfs, as others would visit Buckingham Palace long after General Tom Thumb had left the country.

Barnum finally secured a run of performances at the prestigious Astley's Amphitheatre on Westminster-bridge road. Astley's was the 'home' of British circus, having been founded by Philip Astley in 1768. The Amphitheatre underwent several reincarnations and at the time of Barnum's visit was under the management of William Batty. The General presented *Hop o'my Thumb* as part of the programme and also presented blackface melodies and dances, although there is no direct evidence that he actually 'blacked up' in performance. After completing his engagements at Astley's, he then embarked upon another fairly extensive provincial tour that lasted for the rest of 1846 and into 1847. The tour covered Kent, the south coast towns, Devon, Cornwall, the Midlands, and the northwest of England. Most of the exhibitions were of two or three days, with occasional one-night stands in smaller towns. In major cities like Birmingham and Manchester extended stays were arranged. Wherever he appeared, the General was showered with gifts (and kisses!). In Birmingham he was presented with a pony;

To the Editor of Aris's Gazette

Sir, Before I take my leave of the people of England, from whom I have received so many acts of kindness, I must not omit mentioning that I paid a visit last evening to Hughe's Mammoth Equestrian Establishment and was highly delighted with the entertainments there presented; at the end of which Mr Hughes, in the most handsome manner, presented to me a most beautiful pony, decidedly the smallest I ever beheld, and the most diminutive in that gentleman's extensive group. Such unlooked-for kindness on the part of Mr Hughes will ever be remembered by

Yours &c. GENERAL TOM THUMB
(*Aris's Birmingham Gazette* 1 February 1847)

But this was to be perhaps the last major gift that he would receive. Shortly after this letter was published the following announcement appeared in several British newspapers;

GENERAL TOM THUMB - This illustrious personage, the pet alike of the royalty and commonalty of Europe, embarked on board the Cambria, on Thursday last, on his return from his golden tour to his home in the United States ... He has received many valuable presents from the principal sovereigns of Europe; has kissed more than a million and a half of ladies; has exhibited before 3,000,000 of persons, and the gross receipts of his exhibition exceed £150,000 (*Staffordshire Advertiser* 6 Feb 1847)

Some reports claimed that Stratton had made £100,000 from the tour for himself, while Barnum's profits had been more than this. And all of this in addition to the gifts that had been showered upon them both throughout the tour. The final farewell from the Egyptian Hall was colourfully covered by the *Pictorial Times* and the report needs to be read in full to capture the scene.

The noiseless exit of the celebrated morsel of humanity who, for the last three years, has delighted the female, and vexed the souls of the male, portion of the British public, has rendered people dubious of his departure from our shores. We are, however, enabled to testify to the absolute and melancholy fact, and at the same time to present a faithful illustration of the touching incidents which signalised his final 'adieux'. It is no impeachment of the penny-a-liners that they have not made the readers of daily papers cognisant of the General's flight; they cannot be, as our special reporters are, ubiquitous; nor were they privy to an event which a delicate consideration for the chief actor, or actresses, required should be kept as secret as – anything can be kept in Piccadilly.

Early in the morning previous to the General's departure, Mr Barnum marshalled the *elite* of the guard (consisting of the leading *protectrices* of the interesting *lusus naturae*), in front of the Egyptian Hall. The General being duly apprised of their state of preparation in the form of three sides of a square, drew forth a pocket-handkerchief, presented to him by the Countess of – [sic], and putting on the *chapeau* which identified him with the greatest general of the age, next to our Duke, walked forth unattended into the middle of the street. A burst of sobs, accompanied by pathetic exclamations of 'Oh dear! Oh dear!' greeted the hero as he advanced, and Lady Julia – [sic], unable to control her emotions, rushed forth, and seizing him in her arms, almost drowned him in her gushing tears. One after another of the attached and faithful followers, disregarding the constraints which military discipline imposes upon human feeling, imitated the example of the enthusiastic Julia, and similarly bathed their distinguished and versatile pet. 'Farewell' he said; 'to your egregious passion, my beloved ones, I owe my vast successes; but for your early countenance of one of Nature's freaks, I might have passed through life as unnoticed and undistinguished as the Boshmen [sic] of South Africa, or the 'What is it?' of the Surrey Gardens. *You* sanctioned deformity; *you* hallowed monstrosity; and where *you* lead society at large will follow. Adoo! (we give the exact pronunciation) 'Adoo; remember *me; A-Do*'; saying which he stood on tip-toe and embraced the end of one of the placards embroidered by his most attached follower; and entered his carriage conjugating, 'I calculate, thou calculates (apostrophising Barnum), he calculates, we calculate.' A faint, hysterical cheer issued from the desolate guard, and a forlorn band struck up –

Sigh no more ladies,
Sigh no more,
Men were deceivers ever,

As the diminutive equipage marched up Piccadilly *en route* for Liverpool. It was a touching and instructive sight. We shall not readily forget either the General or his fair admirers (*Pictorial Times* 13 March 1847)

Maybe a somewhat over-sentimentalised account of Stratton's departure from London, though even if it was choreographed by Barnum for maximum publicity, it does contain some thought-provoking words. Whoever was responsible for Tom Thumb's parting words, whether Barnum or Stratton of his own accord, they made a telling point. Stratton, and it certainly has a feeling that this is being spoken from the heart, refers to himself as one of nature's freaks, and as a monstrosity;

*The departure of Tom Thumb (*The Pictorial Times *13 March 1847)*

a deformity. This is something that neither he nor Barnum had mentioned before and there is a feeling of genuine thanks for the way in which the public had embraced Stratton's 'otherness'. Although Barnum may have plucked Stratton from obscurity and exhibited him to the point of exploitation, without public support and interest he may have continued to live his life totally unnoticed. Indeed, the *Carlisle Patriot* of 12 February 1847 gives a resumé of the visit to Europe and his accomplishments;

> ... we would briefly glance at his unparalleled success since his arrival in Europe. He has appeared before more crowned heads than any person living – that is to say, any person in the *exhibition line* ... He speaks French fluently – plays the piano - is learning the violin and other instruments. He played in a French piece in Paris and the principal French cities; was elected member of the

Dramatic Society in Paris; has played Hop o'my Thumb and Bombastes Furioso with great *eclat* in London and elsewhere. He has received many valuable presents from the principal sovereigns in Europe; has kissed more than a million and a half of ladies; has exhibited before 3,000,000 of persons, and the gross receipts of his exhibitions exceed £150,000, which, reckoning 56 sovereigns to the pound avoirdupoise, would make 2,678 pounds weight of gold, and as the General weighs but 15 pounds, it follows that he has received 178 times his own weight in gold! The General has achieved all his triumphs under the direction of P. T. Barnum, Esq., proprietor of the American Museum, New York, who first brought him before the public in America, and who has personally attended him in all his peregrinations. It is gratifying to know that while this gentleman has reaped a rich reward for his enterprise, he has also secured a splendid fortune for his little protégé and parents.

His departure from the port of Liverpool was witnessed by thousands at the dockside and several illustrious persons had made the journey from London to mark his and Barnum's departure. William Batty, manager of Astley's Amphitheatre was there, as well as the director of the Ethiopian Serenaders from St James' Theatre, and the chief superintendent of the principal public exhibitions and amusements in Great Britain. Barnum's golden tour of Europe had come to an end and had taken a little longer than perhaps he had initially planned. It ended as it began, on a Liverpool dockside. The only difference being that his departure was marked with pomp and circumstance, unlike his arrival when he slipped into the country as a little-known American entrepreneur.

Notes

1   *Liverpool Albion* 14 December 1846.

2   Letter #453 8 December 1845.

3   The Adelaide Gallery of Practical Science was an exhibition hall near the Strand in London. It was not always used for scientific exhibitions, as commented upon here; We were somewhat surprised to witness at this place last night a series of exhibitions, we cannot say entertainments, which bear no sort of relation to science either in practice or theory, and which are certainly neither adapted to enlighten an audience nor confer much respectability on the establishment in which they were displayed. There was an elderly and somewhat heavy-looking person whose tedious narrative of old Americanisms was occasionally relieved by the songs of a confederate in his absurdities; this part of the entertainment met with occasional sibilations, and fortunately was finished before the hisses were general. A bell, similar to that used by dustmen, was then rung by a person who announced that, by the payment of an extra 6d. a piece, each lady and gentleman present might inspect the studies and labours of the industrious fleas. Shortly after this, half-a-dozen of that class of persons who are not inappropriately termed "snobs" inhaled the laughing-gas, and managed by the display of various antics to make themselves greater fools than nature perhaps designed them to be. This sort of exhibition may perhaps attract, and fill the pockets of the proprietor of the gallery better than an exhibition of things really and legitimately connected with science; but surely it is too much to call the building in which such scenes are exhibited the "Gallery of Practical Science." (*Dictionary of Victorian London*)

4   A hand is a unit of measurement used in measuring the height of horses. One hand is equal to four inches. In this case, the Mammoth Horse stood at 84 inches at the shoulder (8 feet).

5   *The Scotsman* 31 December 1845.

6   Letter #500 1 January 1846.

7   *Stirling Observer* 5 March 1846.

8   *Illustrated London News* 21 March 1846.

9   Letter #711 31 March 1846.

10 Letter #739 14 May 1846.

11 *Sun (London)* 30 May 1846.

CHAPTER 7 – FAME AND FORTUNE

Barnum's three-year tour of Britain and Europe was to be the first of several further visits that he made to the 'old world' across the Atlantic, all of which came at important moments in his life. Although the 1844 - 1847 tour was pivotal in his life, it is worth briefly considering how his career subsequently developed to understand the reasons for these visits.

When Barnum and his entourage returned home to the USA in February 1847, he must have reflected upon whether his three-year journey had been a success or not. It certainly had been a financial success. The tour had netted him a profit in excess of £100,000, maybe even as much as £150,000 if some reports are accurate. That does not take into account the numerous valuable gifts and money that he had also received during the tour from wealthy benefactors. His American Museum in New York was adding to this wealth while he was out of the country, the daily takings now being more than it previously made in one week. He was also now a land owner, having bought 17 acres of land to the west of Bridgeport, on which he intended to build his estate. To make money from the tour had been one of his goals, but what of expanding his reputation? Barnum was a self-confessed self-publicist, and his name was rarely out of the newspapers on either side of the Atlantic. He craved approbation for himself and his work. The tour of Europe had catapulted him into a figure of international renown. If his name was well known in America before he left for Europe, then on his return it was even more so. As much of an attraction as the American

Museum was, Barnum himself now became an attraction. He records in his autobiography;

> I was surprised to find that I had also become a curiosity during my absence. If I showed myself about the Museum or wherever else I was known, I found eyes peering and fingers pointing at me and could frequently overhear the remark, 'There's Barnum'.

He had added greatly to his extensive array of exhibits at the Museum as a result of the tour. Live animals, stuffed animals, paintings, artefacts, novelty acts such as the 'Swiss' bell-ringers (who in fact were from Lancashire, England)[1], human curiosities—excessively large, small, hirsute people, ethnographic displays, scientific apparatus, and special items such as the state robe worn by Queen Victoria[1] were all on display to the delight of the thousands of visitors who visited his American Museum palace of wonder.

Charles Stratton performing as General Tom Thumb, was also a major beneficiary of the tour. As one of the main attractions of the time, Barnum aimed to promote—some might argue exploit—the diminutive General to his fullest extent. As we have seen, this was done to maximum effect. Charles Stratton returned to America a very wealthy young man of about 10 years, reportedly worth around £100,000. Although, as a minor, the money was held by his father on his behalf.

So, overall, Barnum could bask in the glory of a very successful European tour. One might have expected that after being away from home for three years he would have spent time with his wife and family. But Barnum was something of a workaholic. He immediately put General Tom Thumb on display at the American Museum for four weeks, capitalising on the publicity gained from the tour. This was a huge success and drew vast crowds. After his four-week exhibition, Stratton returned to Bridgeport for a month before beginning an extensive tour of America, with Barnum in attendance. The financial arrangement was as had been agreed in 1845, a 50/50 share of the profits. Barnum the showman was on the road again and in April 1847 he was in Washington DC, where he and Tom Thumb visited President Polk. The tour continued, taking in Richmond, Baltimore, Philadelphia, Boston, Providence, Salem, Springfield, Albany, Niagara Falls and towns in between before ending in New York. In some venues Tom Thumb was exhibited for several days at a time. In Philadelphia, he spent twelve days where the receipts totalled $5,594. He was still making money. By that November, they were in Havana, Cuba before moving on to the American South, ultimately ending up in Pittsburgh, Pennsylvania in May of 1848. It was at this point that Barnum decided to return home, leaving Stratton in the capable hands of his agents.

While he was 'on the road' during 1847, Barnum had instructed a competent architect to begin the construction of his new home on the land that he had bought in 1846. The following notice appeared in the British press;

> HUMBUG PALACE – Mr Barnum, who recently exhibited Tom Thumb in this country, has erected, near New York, a spacious palace, in the eastern style, the piazzas filled with latticework, and the roof and wings surmounted with turrets and minarets. The Americans have named it 'Shingle Palace'. He himself calls it 'Humbug Palace', in allusion to the means whereby he obtained his wealth (*Liverpool Albion* 30 August 1847)

The above suggests that the house had been erected already by this date but in fact it would not be completed until 1848. The design appears very eccentric for an American dwelling but Barnum had been impressed by the architecture of Brighton Pavilion when he had visited that town in England. The Pavilion had been erected for King George IV and had been designed in the oriental style, the only building of its kind in England. There was nothing like it in America and Barnum decided to import the style into creating his own distinctive home that would act as an advertisement to his various ventures. It was near completion in March 1848;

> Mr Barnum's house is nearly completed. The structure, which seems to be a compound of Moorish, Gothic and Turkish architecture attracts a great many visitors. An English gentleman who was here lately, declared that he had come 3,000 miles for the purpose of taking a look at the thing ... We believe there is nothing in England, or indeed in Christendom, resembling this edifice, except the Brighton Pavilion, built by George IV. That is a much larger building, but the model is in almost every respect inferior. There are more expensive houses in the country, but none probably as showy. The cost of the structure and ground will be some 120,000 dollars (*The Pilot* 20 March 1848 – from the *Bridgeport Standard*)

Barnum named this creation Iranistan, meaning loosely 'Persian Home' or 'Oriental Villa'. It was an eclectic collection of eastern architectural styles constructed in three storeys with many arches and porches. The whole structure was surmounted with pinnacle onion domes, truly an exotic appearance for rural Connecticut.

> Elegant and appropriate furniture was made expressly for every room in the house. I erected expensive water-works to supply the premises. The stables, conservatories and out-buildings were perfect in their kind. There was a profusion of trees set out in the

grounds. The whole was built and established literally 'regardless of expense' for I had no desire even to ascertain the entire cost (Benton 1891)

Iranistan (Library of Congress)

No expense was spared in the construction and furnishing of such a magnificent mansion, and I think that the last sentence in the above gives us an indication of Barnum's attitude towards money. Clearly Barnum was wealthy enough not to question the cost of such a venture. He and his family moved into their new home in November 1848, but they were only there for a relatively short period. In 1852 the building was badly damaged by a fire and Barnum set about having it rebuilt. In 1857 a far more disastrous fire broke out and the building was completely destroyed.

With the building of Iranistan it seemed that Barnum was preparing to settle down to a more domestic way of life. But he was a restless soul and continued to add to his American Museum. In July of 1848, while the finishing touches were being put on his new home, he engaged a family of 'mammoth infants';

> Governor Barnum, having cleared one fortune with the smallest man in the creation, is now going the right way to work to get another, with a family of mammoth infants he has procured. They are three in number, two, under eleven years of age, weigh 500 lbs; and the youngest, who has not reached nine months, turns the scale with a half-hundred weight in it (*Lloyd's Weekly Newspaper* 9 July 1848)

He also discovered a dwarf to rival General Tom Thumb;

> Among other curiosities in New York we had the pleasure of seeing at Barnum's ... the greatest of all curiosities, in the smallest of all possible trousers – the renowned human, Major Little Finger ... I can't remember how many inches long, or short, he is or how long it takes to go round him, but this much I well recollect, he is decidedly the smallest specimen of humanity that I ever saw 'walking like a man'. He is much smaller than the General, being only a Major, and much better proportioned. His age is said to be ten years, and the gentleman having him in charge says he was born in London. The ladies all declare he is a 'very proper man', and kisses with quite an unction (*Douglas Jerrold's Weekly Newspaper* 2 Dec 1848 - from the *Boston Chronotype*)

But by far his most adventurous project was in bringing the Swedish vocalist Jenny Lind, known as the 'Swedish Nightingale', to America. She was famous across Europe for her operatic soprano roles. He had not met the woman—nor had he even heard her sing—but her reputation alone was enough to persuade him that there was a potential profit in the venture.

> In October 1849, I first conceived the idea of bringing Jenny Lind to this country ... It struck me, when I first thought of this speculation, that if properly managed it must prove immensely profitable.

It was never going to be an easy project to put into action and there were lengthy discussions between Barnum's agents and those of Jenny Lind. It was also an expensive project for Barnum in that to engage the singer for 150 concerts across America, he would have to advance $187,500 to a London bank. In the end, his advance payments far exceeded this figure as expenses continued to increase. Undeterred, Barnum continued with the project, believing steadfastly that it would be a success. In January 1850, it was announced that Jenny Lind would travel to America.

> We are now enabled to state. On undoubted authority, that 'The Swedish Nightingale' has accepted the offer made to her by Mr Barnum, and that she will proceed to America as soon as the necessary arrangements have been completed ... He (our informant) says that 'he has concluded an engagement with her to give one hundred concerts or oratorios; but she is not to appear in any opera, she having entirely given up the stage.' From another source we learn that Mr Barnum's agent was authorised to offer 250,000 dollars for one hundred and fifty nights and, if that were not sufficient, he was empowered to add an additional 125,000 dollars, making altogether upwards of 88,000l [pounds sterling] or more than 500l for each of the one hundred and fifty times she is to sing ...The only stipulation Jenny Lind has made is, that she shall be at liberty to sing at any time, and as often as she may think fit,

in favour any charitable institution or object (*Freeman's Journal* 25 January 1850)

The only problem for Barnum was that the vast majority of the American public had no idea who Jenny Lind was. As always, he used the newspapers to prime America for her visit. He wrote an open letter from his American Museum that appeared in several American journals. It was a lengthy letter that praised Jenny Lind as 'a lady whose extraordinary vocal powers have never been even approached by any other human being'. A copy of the full letter even appeared in the British press[2]. This seems to have enthused the public for Jenny Lind so that on her arrival in New York on the 1st of September, the scenes of welcome were almost unbelievable. The *New York Herald* covered the event, which was then later published in the *Liverpool Standard* on 17 September;

> The Swedish Nightingale, the soul of song, has at length arrived in the empire city of the great republic of the new world, and her welcome has been cordial and enthusiastic in proportion to her fame ... The Atlantic having been expected on Saturday evening, Mr Barnum proceeded to Staten Island to meet the great songster ... But a storm which the Atlantic encountered in her passage, delayed her for several hours and she did not arrive till Sunday afternoon ... It turned out, however, that she could not conveniently land at Staten Island and many, therefore, were disappointed. On the gallant ship steaming up to the Quarantine, Mr Barnum accompanied the health officer on board, and there met the nightingale, when cordial salutations were exchanged. On seeing the American flag, she paid it homage by kissing her hand to it with all the fervour of a child ... Meantime, the foot of Canal-street was covered with human beings, who had congregated there all day, in expectation of getting

a sight of the Swede; and when the news arrived that the Atlantic was coming up the river, the excitement became intense, and there was a perfect rush, up to the time of her reaching then dock ...all the docks around were covered with men, women and children. There were trains of coaches drawn up in front of the entrance to the dock, the flags of Sweden and the stars and stripes floated on the breeze together ... From the gate halfway up the dock, a beautiful arcade had been erected, consisting of a double row of pillars, festooned with evergreens and flowers, and covered overhead with the flags of the Union ... Here, Mr Barnum's private carriage was drawn up, and from this to the gangway of the ship was extended a carpet for her to walk on ... such was the anxiety for seeing her that many gentlemen climbed up the stakes, at the risk of their lives, and were compelled by the police to come down ... At length Captain West, commanding the Atlantic, appeared with Jenny Lind leaning on his arm, wearing a blue silk bonnet, and having in her hand an exquisite bouquet ... A number, who could not get seeing her, ran forward with precipitation towards the carriage, in order to catch a glimpse of her as she entered; and here the scene baffled all description. The carriage was so surrounded, that it seemed quite impossible for her to get into it. The choicest bouquets were showered upon her, and when with the exertions of those friends who accompanied her, she at length gained the interior of the carriage, the people got up on the horses, while others climbed the carriage roof, and bouquets were thrown to her in profusion ... At this moment was heard a wild hurragh at the gate ... The people who had been kept off with hard fighting by the police, at length made one tremendous rush, carrying the gate in with them, and this heightened the excitement to a pitch of wild tumult ... There appeared to be no hope of getting through the crowd. The driver had only to battle for it; he whipped the horses, which he found to be useless, and then he whipped the crowd.

The carriage with Jenny Lind aboard eventually battled its way through the throng towards Irving House, where another crowd was waiting to catch a glimpse of her. What a welcome! And although it is recorded that Jenny Lind graciously acknowledged the crowd's enthusiastic welcome, she surely must have wondered as to what exactly she had let herself in for.

Jenny Lind mania swept the country. People flocked to her concerts and Jenny Lind merchandise was all the rage. There were Jenny Lind bonnets, riding hats, shawls, robes, gloves etc—all for sale for a price. Over the course of the next 10 months, the Swedish Nightingale gave 95 concerts around the country, including Havana. Occasionally there had been moments of controversy and Barnum had been forced to issue a statement refuting Lind's alleged donation to the Abolitionist Movement[3]. He feared that such a rumour would damage Lind's appearances in the south. A letter in *The Liberator* of December 1850 demanded of Barnum,

> I understand that there is an insidious report in secret circulation, calculated, if not designed, to injure the success of M'lle Lind in this city and in the South. It is insinuated that, besides the acts of beneficence which she has conferred on our countrymen, and which do her so much honor, she has presented an association of abolitionists in the North with one thousand dollars, for the purpose of promoting their alarming and detestable projects. Do me the favor to say whether this report is not without the slightest foundation.

Jenny Lind 1850 (Library of Congress)

She had been engaged by Barnum for 100 concerts but she had paid him an agreed forfeit to close the tour prematurely. Overall, the tour had been a great success and Barnum's gamble had paid off. He records that his gross receipts, after paying Jenny Lind, was $535,486.

With all this accrued wealth one might wonder why it was, a few years later, that Barnum found himself facing bankruptcy. Always being attracted to new ideas, he embarked upon several other projects during this time. He set up and toured 'Barnum's Great Asiatic Caravan, Museum and Menagerie'. It was a large-scale travelling exhibition that included the Grand State carriage of the late Dowager Queen of England. He became editor of the Bridgeport based newspaper the *Illustrated News* and invited the English novelist William Makepeace Thackeray, famous for *Vanity Fair*, to contribute an article to the first edition—something he declined. He completed the first version of his autobiography which sold over a million copies in its various revisions. He became involved in the Crystal Palace Company to build a grander version of London's Crystal Palace for the exhibition of the Industry of All Nations. And, ill-fatedly, he made loans to the Jerome Clock Company—a company that ultimately failed, wiping out all of Barnum's wealth. Fortunately, he had signed over the lease of the Museum to his wife but almost everything else was lost. As he wrote, somewhat phlegmatically;

> The clocks folk have wound me up. Never mind. My wife owns the Museum lease, which will give her an annual income for the next 23 years that will support us (Saxon: Letter 74 p91)

A report in the *New York Herald* appeared in the British press.

> The author of that book glorifying himself as a millionaire from the arts and appliances of obtaining money under false pretences,

is, according to his own statement in court, completely crushed out. All the profits of all his Feejee mermaids, all his woolly horses, Greenland whales, Joyce Hethes [sic], negroes turning white, Tom Thumbs, and monsters and imposters of all kinds, including 70,000 dollars received for the copyright of that book are all swept away, Hindoo palace, elephants and all by the late invincible showman's remorseless assignees ... the whole community will be pleased to learn that in spirit he is not broken down, but that he has yet the activity required to start with the world again in a less ostentatious but more honourable business career than that which made him a Jeremy Diddler, a mountebank, a millionaire, and a bankrupt (*People's Paper* 19 April 1856)

It was a disastrous time. He had lost his fortune, his home was now shut up, his family were living in rented rooms, and his immediate prospects looked bleak. Barnum had been out-Barnumed! But he was as resolute as ever and looked to the future. It was to be Jenny Lind and Charles Stratton who helped him at his time of need. Lind offered a sum of money to assist him and Stratton offered his support and proposed another visit to London and Europe—almost 10 years after his first visit. And so, this is how Barnum came to make a return trip to England, and one that would result in a major change in his later life.

Barnum's arrival in Liverpool in December of 1856 was very low key. In fact, it was General Tom Thumb who captured the headlines—Barnum was merely a footnote in the report[4]. At the General's exhibitions in London, Barnum was described as a 'visitor' and although he accompanied Stratton on several of his visits around London, he did not command the attention that he did previously. It took a letter to the press from C L West, the agent for Tom Thumb, to clarify the situation;

As for Mr Barnum, he has no connection whatever with the general who, accompanied by his mother [Stratton Snr. was dead by this time] and other members of the family, is travelling solely on his own account (*Atlas* 17 January 1857)

Ostensibly, Barnum's prime reason for being in England was to promote the Howard family of actors, mother, father, and daughter, in their production of *Uncle Tom's Cabin*. Stratton was pursuing his own career, albeit with agents sponsored by Barnum. But this was not the whole truth. As ever, Barnum was on the lookout to make money, especially under his current position. He was deliberately playing down his involvement with the General's exhibitions, as he explained;

These were strong spokes in the wheel that was moving strongly but surely in the effort to get me out of debt, and, if possible, to save some portion of my real estate. Of course, it was not generally known that I had any interest whatever in either of these exhibitions; if it had been, possibly some of the clock creditors would have annoyed me; but I busied myself in these and other ways, working industriously and making much money, which I constantly remitted to my trusted agent at home (Barnum 1886:159)

Of course, he was also always on the lookout for exhibition material for his museum and was reported to have offered $1,000 for a hogshead (a 150-gallon container) of London Colonial Gin. This was in contradiction to his having 'taken the pledge and drinking no alcohol. He became an avid member of the Temperance Movement.He was also reinventing himself as a lecturer on abstaining from alcohol. He lectured throughout England on the 'Maine Liquor Law', which was an act prohibiting the sale of alcohol for general consumption. He also presented lectures on the subject of 'making money', which were well received.

It was during this visit to England that he made the acquaintance of John Fish, a cotton mill owner and self-made man. He looked upon Barnum as a mentor and invited him on several occasions to his home in Southport. It was here that he met Nancy Fish, the nine-year-old daughter of John. Barnum became a firm friend of the family and regularly communicated by letter with both John and Nancy. Indeed, both John and Nancy later visited Barnum in America and stayed for several months as his guests while they toured the country. It was a friendship that would have a significant effect on his life in later years.

Barnum's 'unofficial' exhibitions of General Tom Thumb in England during 1856 and 1857, as well as his lecture tours generated a significant amount of money. That, and with the help of some friends who had helped to buy up his liabilities, allowed him to prepare to take repossession of his home, Iranistan. Unfortunately, not long after his return, and before the family could move in, the house was destroyed in a disastrous fire in December 1857. Iranistan was never rebuilt in its former glory, but Barnum commissioned a new home in 1860 to be built near that of his daughter Caroline. This he named Lindencroft and it was built in the Italianate style. He would later build a third home near the sea in 1869, Waldemere, so that his ailing wife could follow medical advice to breathe in sea air. His tours with the General in 1858 and 1859, taking them across Germany and Holland, began to rebuild his wealth.

The destruction of Iranistan had been the second fire to affect the house, and it was fire that seemed to dog Barnum from this point on. In 1865 the American Museum burned down. After the fire he wrote to Bayard Taylor;

> There's no disputing the fact that the destruction of the Museum is a national loss ... But the next one must be of a much higher grade ... It will be a vast building with every accommodation, immense lecture room on ground floor (rear) where I can trot in circus horses 12 weeks every winter, a picture gallery, a hall for statuary, full collection of specimens of natural history in all its departments, and on the roof a zoological garden reached by the screw elevator ride ... (Saxon. Letter 119 p136)

This was rebuilt and opened only several months later, and Barnum had the idea of approaching all the major museums across Europe to

Lindencroft 1864 (Library of Congress)

make donations of exhibits to the new museum. Charles Stratton, now married to Lavinia Warren[5], was again an instrumental benefactor to the project. Tragically, the rebuilt museum too was consumed by fire in March of 1868 and Barnum took the decision to 'retire'.

The words 'Barnum' and 'retire' do not sit easily together. His serious musical project with Jenny Lind and his commitment to the Temperance Movement might indicate that he was attempting a more respectable image, preparing to become more of a model citizen and less of a travelling showman. Perhaps even his bankruptcy may have been something of a salutary experience. But Barnum could not easily settle to a life of domesticity. Indeed, from the 1850s onwards during the following three decades, he was four times in the Connecticut legislature, ran for Congress, and the Senate, albeit unsuccessfully. He served a term of office as the Mayor of Bridgeport. He was involved in opposition to the railroad interest in the state and was a leader in the

General Tom Thumb and wife Lavinnia Warren (central pair), with Commodore Nutt and Miss Minnie Warren. 1865 CdV (Author's collection)

movement to grant the vote to negroes. The epitome of progressive respectability—but the showman was still there inside him.

By 1871, he had formed and was touring 'P. T. Barnum's Museum, Menagerie and Circus', opening under canvas in Brooklyn before moving to the Empire Rink in New York City. In the following year he bought the Hippotheatron, a building originally constructed as the New York Circus in 1864. It was polyhedral in shape and modelled on the Cirque Napoleon in Paris. Remodelled and improved over the years, the building took on its Hippotheatron name in 1869. As we have seen earlier, fires seem to have been the bane of Barnum's life and in December 1872, the Hippotheatron was consumed by flames and his entire stock of animals lost, as well as costumes and belongings of the performers.

> In New York, on the 25th ult., Barnum's Museum [the Hippotheatron] and other buildings were wholly destroyed. The entire collection of wild animals were [sic] burned to death. As the flames reached the cages of wild animals, the screams were fearful. The keepers were unable to allow them to escape, and they were literally roasted alive in their dens. The flames spread to other buildings, to save which all the attention of the firemen had to be directed (*Leicester Daily Post* 4 January 1873)

He immediately bounced back from this disaster and began putting together another mammoth travelling exhibition that he intended to tour throughout the United States; 'Barnum's Travelling World Fair'. But by the autumn he was back in Europe, searching for animals and other such exhibits. It was while he was in Germany that he received news that would change his life. Later, in December, he wrote to John Greenwood in America from London;

> On 20th Nov. I recd. A cable at Hamburg saying my wife died 19th.
> She was paralysed 18th, lay unconscious and died without pain next
> day. I was fast recovering my health, but this set me back. I have
> only averaged 4 hours sleep per night since, until the last 2 nights.
> I remain here 10 days & then go to Italy accompanied by friends.
> I expect to return home March or April (Saxon. Letter 151 p178)

This has always struck me as a strange response to the news of his wife's death. Charity had been ill on and off for many years. When he was first in Europe in the 1840s, he wrote of her illness and again in 1859[6]. Throughout their married life, Barnum was a frequent absentee and yet professed to be a loving husband. He wrote a seemingly heartfelt response to his wife's death in the 1886 edition of his autobiography[7];

> ... the sorrowing husband four thousand miles away from the bedside
> of his dead wife ... When he reflects that children, grandchildren
> and other kindred are mourning over the coffin where he is needed,
> and where his poor stricken heart is beckoning to be ...

Admittedly, it would have taken a while to make the journey from Hamburg to America but transatlantic travel was not an impossibility, even during the winter months, and I am sure that Barnum *could* have made the journey home if he had really wanted to. But what did he do? He first retired to the Southport home of John Fish and found solace in the company of his friend Nancy, now 23 years old. Indeed, they were the friends that he alludes to in the letter to John Greenwood. In the final event he did not travel to Italy but was in London in February 'due to business'. One may wonder what this business was because

Nancy Fish (Public domain image)

there is a record of a marriage between Nancy Fish and Phineas Taylor Barnum on Valentine's Day in 1874[8]. She was not yet 24 years old and he was approaching 64. It begs a question as to what their relationship over the years was—not to mention why they married so soon after Charity's death. Wright (2018) makes an interesting and thought-provoking observation;

> PTB [Phineas Taylor Barnum] had actually been corresponding with Nancy for a long time – as a pen-pal, writing numerous letters over many years. They had begun a friendship long before Charity died, and they even travelled together in Europe ... Sometimes Barnum would take over the entire floor at the top of a hotel, other times apartments with adjoining doors, and they would often play at or 'pretend' to be married.

The implication of Wright's comment is that the pair were conducting an extra-marital affair before Charity died. However, Kathleen Maher, the Director of the Barnum Museum maintains that this was not the case and that the relationship had been completely platonic. Barnum was quite a devout person and upheld the institution of marriage, even if his and Charity's relationship had drifted apart over the years. He had known Nancy for several years and maybe their marriage was for a continued companionship. Another factor is that Barnum was very much a public figure and if there had been the slightest hint of impropriety or scandal, the press would have jumped on it immediately. There is no record in either the British or American press that alludes to this. Of course, one might question Nancy's motivation in marrying a man 40 years her senior. Was it for companionship, love, or did she see Barnum as a means of advancing herself? Certainly, she became a wealthy widow when Barnum later died. The *San Francisco Call* of March 9th 1896 reported that;

> At the death of the veteran showman he left his widow $100,000, Marina, the beautiful home in this city, and an annuity of $40,000 a year.

She went on to marry a reputedly wealthy Greek diplomat by the name of Demitrius Callias. After he died, she then remarried to a French nobleman, the Baron d'Alexandry d'Orengiani. For a provincial young Englishwoman, she had moved in high circles.

Barnum returned to America without his secret bride as he had yet to announce the marriage to his family. She joined him later and they were married (again), quite simply on the 17 September, as described here;

> The *New York Herald* on the 17th inst. says – During the brief interval that followed the close of the morning session of the Universalist Convention yesterday, before the people had time to disperse, a commotion was noticed in the Church of the Divine Paternity ... The organist struck up a wedding quickstep, and rumour carried the news around that P. T. Barnum, the showman, had caught a pretty English Fish and was about to make her his own according to law and custom ... The bride was dressed in a slate-coloured dress and wore a black velvet hat with blue feathers.

From her ears depended diamond earrings. The bridegroom was attired in an evening dress suit. The knot was tied in short order by Dr Chapin ... The couple immediately retired to the Windsor Hotel, where they are at present domiciled. There was no nonsense or ostentation about the wedding ... (*Evening Express* 30 September 1874)

No mention of the previous marriage in England—and the bride didn't wear white! And it is interesting that for a man who craved publicity, the wedding passed off with barely any recognition at all. However, it seems the marriage was well conceived and Barnum settled down to life with his new wife, at first in his home Waldemere, and later in a newly constructed home named Marina—although he still was as busy as ever with various schemes and projects. His Hippodrome was doing well and his mammoth touring show was taking on the title of 'The Greatest Show on Earth'. By now, he was moving the outfit from venue to venue by railroad.

His greatest competition came from the 'Great London Circus, Sanger's Royal British Menagerie and Grand International Allied Shows'. The managers were Messrs. Cooper, Bailey, and Hutchinson. Barnum approached them and after lengthy negotiations it was agreed to combine the two shows into one giant combination, eventually to become known as the 'Barnum & Bailey Circus'. His new partners were to be James Bailey and James Hutchinson. It was a risky business, but risk was something that Barnum could embrace. During 1880, the partnership agreed to build a huge winter quarters on a ten-acre site in Bridgeport adjacent to the New York, New Haven and Hartford railway. This would house all of the wild animals, horses, chariots, railroad cars, and all the equipment of the combined shows. Although fascinated by

Marina. 188 architect's drawing (Library of Congress)

Nº 6. - Vue à vol d'oiseau de la Cité des Tentes de BARNUM & BAILEY.

Barnum & Bailey's vast tented circus. Postcard c.1900 (Author's collection)

this 'city of wonders', the public were denied entry and had to wait until March 1881 to see the 'Barnum & London Circus', which opened at Madison Square Garden on March 28. The *New York Herald* gave this coverage of the opening;

MADISON SQUARE GARDEN –
BARNUM'S CIRCUS AND SHOW

The management at Madison Square Garden have redeemed their promise to give the public one of the best arenic exhibitions in connection with a menagerie that ever has been witnessed in New York. Long before the doors were opened they were besieged by anxious hundreds, and at a quarter past eight o'clock there was scarcely a seat to be obtained in the vast edifice. It was stated by one of the proprietors that about nine thousand persons were present, and fully three thousand who could not be accommodated were refused admission ... Each individual was provided with a chair, so that all crowding was avoided, while an ample supply of ushers promptly and without confusion conducted the holders of tickets to their respective places ... The only drawback to the performance was that the spectator was compelled to receive more than his money's worth; in other words, that while his head was turned in one direction he felt that he was losing something good in another. Three rings were provided, marked on the programmes as Circle No. 1, No. 2 and No. 3; the equestrianism taking place in the two outer rings and the central space being reserved more especially for what are technically known as 'ground acts'.

The piece goes on to detail some of the elements of the show, including an appearance by General Tom Thumb and other human curiosities, a host of wild animals, equestrianism, gymnastic and athletic exercises, trapeze displays, and clowns. For the next 32 weeks the show travelled, according to Barnum, some 12,000 miles, from Bay City, Michigan in the north to Galveston, Texas in the south before returning to its winter quarters in Bridgeport. The show re-opened for a new season in March 1882 at Madison Square Garden.

As part of the 1882 show, Barnum exhibited an enormous African elephant named Jumbo. He had purchased the animal from the Zoological Society of London and had it shipped to America at his own expense. He went on to tour with the beast throughout North America for three years until it was tragically killed in a railway accident near the Canadian town of St. Thomas. Jumbo, or rather the stuffed remains of the animal, would make a return to London in 1889. Barnum's crowning glory and his last visit to England took place that year when he shipped the entire outfit of his 'Greatest Show on Earth' to London. The *Westminster & Pimlico News* gave an account of how the venue had had to be altered to accommodate such a large outfit as well as some facts and figures.

> At the lowest estimate fully 500,000 dollars will be expended by Messrs. Barnum and Bailey before their Greatest Show on Earth gives its opening performance. Several of the largest steamers afloat were required to transport it. It will employ   fully 1,200 people, 380 horses and whole herds and caravans of wild beasts; the classic scenery, costumes and armour used will cost over 75,000 dollars, and its current daily expenses will be fully 6,800 dollars We believe that the hire of the hall alone means something like an outlay of £1,000 a month, and the structural alterations absorb several thousands (*Westminster & Pimlico News* 9 November 1889)

But Barnum's show was supported by a vast exhibition, known as 'Barnum's Museum of Living Curiosities'. A reporter gave this account of a visit to Olympia.

> Entering on Monday night by the door nearest to the Addison-street Station, I was glad to renew acquaintance in the first place with our old elephantine friend Jumbo, albeit there were but the skeleton and the stuffed frame of the former King of the 'Zoo' ... When you have done smiling at the vanity of the 'Skeleton Dude', there's a pocket dwarf to admire, and a brace of giants to gaze at. Here are the Aztecs again, a group of warlike Zulus, a 'Strong Man' of the Samson type, Albinos of radiant beauty, and human wonders to excite curiosity in every direction (*Penny Illustrated Paper* 16 November 1889)

And of the show itself, this was written;

> Certainly, nothing like it in extent and concentrated variety has ever before been seen in England – or, indeed, in Europe. Its fault is that of a bewildering superabundance. As far as the hippodromic portion of the exhibition is concerned, it consists not of one show but of three, in each of which the ordinary circus feats are doubled, and the eye is fatigued in the endeavour to follow all that is going on (*Sleaford Gazette* 23 November 1889)

Barnum himself made an appearance at the beginning of every show, being driven around the arena in a carriage to the applause and cheering of the thousands of spectators. It was a triumphant return to centre stage in London. He returned to America in the spring of the following year and there acquired another circus, Forepaugh's Circus, which he operated as a separate outfit. He was now truly a giant of

The Barnum Institute. Postcard c.1910 (Author's collection)

the entertainment business and he was extremely wealthy. As well as the circuses that he now owned, or had shares in, he was also a man of property. A report was given in 1884 of his holdings;

> The European agent of Barnum has given information concerning the showman's property. During 1882, with his two partners, Barnum cleared $800,000, and the year previous $550,000 by the shows ... Barnum is a stock-holder in two sewing-machine companies, owns three newspapers, two of which are in Bridgeport, about four hundred houses, numerous vacant lots and a cattle ranch. He has one thousand vacant lots In Denver. A building owned by him in New York pays him a rental of $65,000 a year (*American Register* 9 February 1884)

But perhaps at the height of his career, time was gradually running out for Barnum. Early in 1891 he approved plans for a Barnum Institute of Science and History to be built in Bridgeport. He had bequeathed

$100,000 for the building. But Barnum never saw its completion. He died from a stroke on 7 April 1891 at his home in Bridgeport. The Institute was completed in 1893 and is now home to the Barnum Museum. His death was widely lamented and lengthily reported.

EXIT BARNUM

The showman of the century is dead. The man whose portrait beamed down upon us from every street hoarding only some eighteen months ago, has passed out into the shadow of the great beyond. It seems a strange thing to think of the world without Barnum. For over forty years his name has been a household word. Everybody had heard of him, and there were thousands who regarded him in a public way as a private friend ... He leaves behind him many pleasant memories. He was a humbug; he liked to delude the people, but he did it so good naturedly that it became a positive pleasure. From first to last he was a colossal showman, such as the world may not see again for many, many years (Birmingham Mail 8 April 1891)

But perhaps we should allow Barnum himself to have the last word;

As a general thing I have not 'duped the world', nor attempted to do so; but while I do not attempt to justify all I have done, I know that I have generally given to people *the worth of their money twice told*. The Mermaid, Woolly Horse, Ploughing Elephants, &c., were merely used by me as skyrockets or advertisements, to attract attention and give notoriety to the Museum & such other really valuable attractions as I provided for the public. I believe hugely in advertising and blowing my own trumpet, beating the gongs, drums &c., to attract attention to a show; but I never believed that any amount of advertising or energy would make a spurious article permanently successful. No man really believes less in shows than myself. I should dislike to be thought so poor a student of human nature as to believe that money can be made from the public without giving a full equivalent therefor. I don't believe in 'duping the public' but I believe in first attracting and then pleasing them (Saxon. Letter 85 p103)

The Barnum Memorial. Bridgeport, Connecticut. Postcard (Author's collection)

Notes

1   *Selected Letters of P T Barnum*. Ed. A. H. Saxon 1983. Columbia University Press. Letter 19 p25.

2   *Sun (London)* 7 March 1850.

3   Saxon 1983, Op. Cit. Letter 37 p52.

4   *Aris's Birmingham Gazette* 29 December 1856.

5   Charles Stratton married Lavinia Warren, who was also a dwarf under the management of Barnum, on February 10, 1863, at Grace Episcopal Church, New York. Barnum sold tickets for their wedding reception for $75 to the first 5000 applicants. Warren had been romantically pursued by George 'Commodore' Nutt; another dwarf performer employed by Barnum. He was Stratton's best man at the wedding and toured the world with the Strattons and Warren's sister. Minnie.

6   Saxon 1983. Op. Cit. Letter84 p102.

7   Barnum, P. T. 1886. *Life of P. T. Barnum*. Courier Company Printers. Buffalo p288.

8   England and Wales Civil Registration Marriage Index 1837 – 1915. Strand. London. Ref;1b/688. Jan Q 1874. Online at www.ancestry.co.uk

9   *The Times* 25 January 1882.

SELECT BIBLIOGRAPHY

Barnum, P. T. (1855) *The Life of P.T. Barnum. Written by himself.* Redfield, New York

Barnum, P. T. (1869) *Struggles and Triumphs; Or, Forty Years' Recollections of P. T. Barnum.* Reprint 1981. Penguin Publishing Group

Barnum, P. T. (1886) *Life of P. T. Barnum.* Courier Company Printers. Buffalo

Benton, J. (1891) *A Unique Story of a Marvellous Career. Life of Hon. Phineas T. Barnum.* Edgewood Publishing Company

Blanchard, P. et al (ed.) (2008) *Human Zoos; Science and spectacle in the age of colonial empires.* Liverpool University Press

Darby, N. (2017) *Life on the Victorian Stage.* Pen & Sword

Falk, V. (2012) *Fear and Loathing in Nineteenth Century England; Monsters, Freaks, and Deformities and Their Influence on Romantic and Victorian Society.* M.A. Dissertation. Seton Hall University

Fitzsimons, R. (1969) *Barnum in London.* Geoffrey Bles. London

Freeman, H. (2016) *War of 1812.* Hourly History Ltd

Frith, S. (2005) Searching for Sara Bartmann. John Hopkins Magazine. June 2005. Online at; Johns Hopkins Magazine (jh.edu)

Hornberger, F. (2005) *Carny Folk.* Citadel Press

Hunt, M. (1942) *Have you seen Tom Thumb?* J.B. Lippincott Company

Lindfors, B. (1984) *P. T. Barnum and Africa.* Studies in Popular Culture Vol 7 (1984). Popular Cultural Association in the South

Nardinelli, C. (1980) *Child Labour and the Factory Acts.* The Journal of Economic History. Vol. 40, No.4

Reiss, B. (1999) *P. T. Barnum, Joice Heth and Antebellum Spectacles of Race.* American Quarterly, Vol. 51, No. 1 (March 1999) John Hopkins University Press

Sanger, G. (1935) *Seventy Years a Showman.* E. P. Dutton & Co.

Saxon, A.H. Ed. (1983) *Selected Letters of P. T. Barnum.* Columbia University Press

Scot R. (1584) Reprint 1972. *The Discoverie of Witchcraft.* Dover Publications Inc. New York

Sergent, A. (1951) *Barnum; Roi du Bluff.* Pierre Horay

Thompson, E.P. (1963) *The Making of the English Working Class.* New York

Tromp, M. Ed. (2008) *Victorian Freaks.* Ohio State University Press

Ward, S. 2021. *Jumbo the Elephant; a very Victorian institution.* In the Journal of Victorian Culture Online. www.jvc.oup.com/2021/04/08/jumbo-the-elephant/

Washington, H.A. (2006) *Medical Apartheid; The Dark History of Medical Experimentation on Black Americans from Colonial Times to the Present.* Achor Books. New York ps86-89

Woodward. W. (2012) *The War Connecticut Hated.* In Connecticut Explored Vol.10/No. 3 Summer 2012. Online at; https://Connecticuthistory.org/the-war-connecticut-hated/

Woolf, J. (2019) *The Wonders. Lifting the Curtain on the Freak Show, Circus and Victorian Age.* Michael O'Mara Books Ltd.

Wright, G. (2018) *Southport's Nancy Fish married into wealth and fame with 'The Greatest Showman '.* In the Southport Visitor. Online at www.southportvisiter.co.uk

Wright, J. (2018) *How the public autopsy of a slave Joice Heth launched P. T. Barnum's career as the Greatest Showman on Earth.* Clin Anat. 2018 Oct 31 956-965

GENERAL NOTES

In researching this book, a variety of Archives have been consulted, both physically and online:

The National Fairground and Circus Archive. Western Bank Library, Sheffield, S10 2RN, UK and online at https://www. sheffield.ac.uk/nfca

The National Archive. Kew, Richmond, TW9 4DU, UK and online at https://nationalarchives.gov.uk

The Royal Archives. Windsor Castle and online at https://www. royal.uk/the-royal-archives

Westminster Archives. 10 St Anne's Street, London SW1P 2DE and online at www.westminster.gov.uk

The British Library. 96 Euston Road, London, NW1 2DB, UK and online at https://www.bl.uk

The British Library Newspaper Archive at Boston Spa. Thorpe Arch Park, Wetherby, LS23 7BQ, UK and online at https://www. britishnewspaperarchive.co.uk

The Bibliothèque Nationale de France in Paris and online at https://www.bnf.fr/en/gallica-bnf-digital-library

The Library of Congress online at https://www.loc.gov
The Connecticut Digital Archive online at https://ctdigitalarchive.
org

The Barnum Museum online at https://barnum-museum.org

Throughout the book international indicators for monetary units have been used, so GBP for British pounds (£) and USD for American dollars ($). Some readers may be unfamiliar with pre-decimal British money. Prior to 1971, the pound (£) was divided into twenty shillings (s) and each shilling into twelve pence (d). So, 12d = 1s and 20s = £1. There is another unit that is sometimes mentioned, and that is the Guinea. A Guinea was worth twenty-one shillings.

It is often difficult to give accurate conversion values for the period covered in this book. Using the monetary computation and converter website https://www.measuringwealth.com for the median year of 1845 gives an average conversion value of £1 equal to $4.87. As a point of reference, in 2023 £1 was equal to $1.24.

Every effort has been made by the author to locate the copyright holders of images reproduced within this book.

INDEX

E

F

G

H

I

J

K

T

W

ABOUT THE AUTHOR

Steve Ward has a background in theatre and clowning. Moving into teaching, he soon recognised that as well as an artistic activity circus could play an important role in the educational and social development of young people. From his early days in experimenting with circus in the classroom, and projects linking the professional circus, schools, and youth groups he went on to establish his own award-winning youth circus, as well as founding the original National Association of Youth Circus in the UK. Steve has created and directed many youth circus festivals in the UK, as well as in Germany and Brazil.

With a deep-rooted interest in the circus, he now researches and writes about its fascinating cultural history. He has a PhD in Social History by Published Works from the University of Hull, and is a member of the Circus Research Network and the Circus Arts Research Platform, both international organisations. Steve also talks and lectures on aspects of circus history, and has appeared on television and in many radio interviews. He also advises on educational and youth circus matters—and he still finds time to occasionally perform as a clown!

His previous Circus publications are;

Beneath the Big Top; A Social History of the Circus in Britain, Pen & Sword 2014

Sawdust Sisterhood; How Circus Empowered Women, Fonthill Media 2016

Father of the Modern Circus; Billy Buttons; The life & times of Philip Astley, Pen & Sword 2018

Circus Notes & Jottings, Amazon 2017

Nineteenth Century Circus Poster Art, Amazon 2018

Artistes of Colour; Ethnic Diversity and Representation in the Victorian Circus, Modern Vaudeville Press 2021

The Victorian Circuses of Leeds; A Guided Walk, Amazon 2021

Opulence & Ostentation; Building the Circus, Modern Vaudeville Press 2023

Other books by Steve Ward

Robin's Wood, Createspace Publishing Platform 2013 (as Stephen Ward)

The Indentured Man, Createspace Publishing Platform 2014 (as Stephen Ward)

Tales from the Big House; Temple Newsam, Pen & Sword 2017

OTHER BOOKS BY MODERN VAUDEVILLE PRESS

Juggling: Or How to Become a Juggler (annotated edition)

Rupert Ingalese, annotated by Thom Wall
ISBN – 978-1733971201
99 pages
MSRP: $15 USD

The fully annotated edition of Rupert Ingalese's 1921 "how to juggle" manual. This book covers basic juggling technique, tricks with hats and canes, practice methodology, and more. Ingalese's manuscript provides an interesting look at the state of juggling pedagogy in Britain's music hall era. Annotations by juggler and circus researcher Thom Wall bring insight and context to Ingalese's descriptions and instructions.

Pottery in Motion

Sam Veale
ISBN – 978-1733971232
71 pages
MSRP: $15 USD

British juggler Sam Veale's *Pottery in Motion* is the first of its kind - a straightforward book that provides aspiring plate spinners both the specifics of the props (such as plates, sticks, and rack) and comprehensive instruction on the skill of plate spinning itself. This small but detail-packed guide appeals to individuals looking to learn plate spinning and provides the knowledge to take it to a performance-ready level, just add practice.

Juggling: From Antiquity to the Middle Ages

Thom Wall
ISBN – 978-0578410845
129 pages
MSRP: $25 USD

As with dance, so with juggling—the moment that the performer finishes the routine, their act ceases to exist beyond the memory of the audience. There is no permanent record of what transpired, so studying the ancient roots of juggling is fraught with difficulty. Using the records that do exist, juggling appears to have emerged around the world in cultures independent of one another in the ancient past. Paintings in Egypt from 2000 BCE show jugglers engaged in performance. Stories from the island nation of Tonga place juggling's creation with their goddess of the underworld—a figure who has guarded a cave since time immemorial. Juggling games and rituals are pervasive in isolated Inuit cultures in northern Canada and Greenland. Though the earliest representation of juggling is 4,000 years old, the practice is surely much older—in the same way that humans were doubtlessly singing and dancing long before the first bone flute was created.

This book is an attempt to catalogue this tangible history of juggling in human culture. It is the story of juggling, represented in art and writing from around the world, across time. Although much has been written about modern jugglers–specific performers, their props, and their routines–little has been said about those who first developed the craft. As juggling enters a golden age in the internet era, *Juggling: From Antiquity to the Middle Ages* offers a look into the past—to the origins of our art form.

Spanish Edition:

Malabares - desde la Antigüedad hasta la Edad Media: la historia olvidada de lanzar y cachar

Thom Wall, et. al.
ISBN – 978-1733971263
179 pages
MSRP: $25 USD

Malabares - desde Antigüedad hasta la Edad Media, es un divertido viaje por países, por épocas. Desde el Antiguo Egipto y sus ya famosas malabaristas profesionales de la tumba nº 15 de Beni Hasan, a los juegos para niñas de la isla de Tonga y otras zonas del Pacífico Sur; pasando por los edictos del rey Alfonso X de Castilla sobre la regulación de los juglares o los antipodistas aztecas actuando ante el Papa Clemente VII en el siglo XVI. También reserva un espacio al final del libro para, aprovechando su faceta de lingüista, realizar unas reflexiones acerca de la propia definición de la palabra "juggling"[malabarismo] a lo largo del tiempo y sus orígenes. Es, por tanto, un libro ideal no solo para malabaristas o cirqueros, sino para cualquiera con curiosidad sobre la historia, en especial de aquellos hechos que en ocasiones pasan más desapercibidos en los textos cotidianos.

A través de este libro aprendemos sobre leyendas y juegos antiguos, fantaseamos con grandes artistas y actuaciones que nunca podremos ver y que nos hacen dudar sobre esa tan manida sentencia que a veces afirma "esto nunca se ha hecho antes".
- Malabares en su Tinta

Juggling: What It Is and How to Do It

Thom Wall, et. al.
ISBN – 978-1-7339712-5-6
224 pages
MSRP: $25 USD

  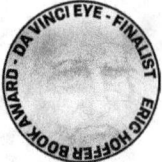

Juggling: What It Is and How to Do It teaches learners of all ages how to juggle – one of the world's oldest artforms. With a kind demeanor, humor, and enthusiasm, this authoritative manual explains the process of juggling through four different modalities, bolstered by the latest physical education research.

Juggling is an accessible primer that a middle-schooler can hit the ground running with, or that families can enjoy together. The result of six years of work by 2021 International Jugglers' Association *Excellence in Education* award winner and former Cirque du Soleil juggler Thom Wall and featuring guest chapters by some of today's juggling masters, *Juggling* provides great content for even the most serious adult learner.

Book plus Juggling Kit!

Includes juggling balls by Alchemy Juggling

MSRP: $60 USD

This exclusive kit makes the perfect gift for any aspiring juggler. Includes one copy of *Juggling: What It Is and How to Do It* and three professional-grade beanbags.

Beanbag specs: 90g ea., approx. 2.75" diameter. Machine washable / dryable. Made in USA.

Body Talk: *Basic Mime*

Mario Diamond
ISBN – 978-1733971218
73 pages
MSRP: $15 USD

Body Talk: Basic Mime covers the fundamental skills of mime in an easily accessible workbook format. Diamond brings over 40 years of teaching and performance experience to *Body Talk*, which includes rich photography illustrating various mime techniques.

"[*Body Talk: Basic Mime*] should be required reading for any theater participant looking to incorporate elements of mime into their routines." - *Midwest Book Review*

French Edition: *Corps Expressif: Base du Mime*

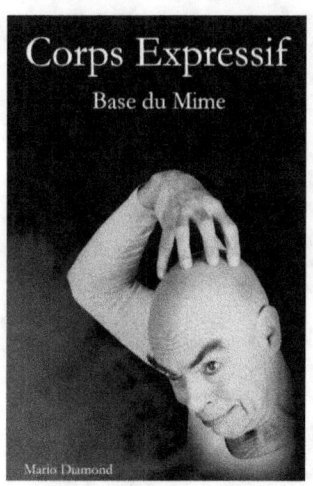

Mario Diamond
ISBN – 978-1958604984
68 pages
MSRP: $15 USD

Mario a écrit un tour de force sur l'art du mime. Ce livre est éloquent et concis... riche en outils pour les élèves comme pour les professeurs, facile à comprendre et rempli d'exercices pratiques. Ce livre est brodé de segments historiques et anecdotiques qui en font un manuscrit amusant, plein d'observations charmantes et bouffonnes qui font de Mario un artiste phénoménal, prodigue de la caractéristique définitive du mime, la personnalité.

Circus Games (v1.1)

Compiled by Lucy Little & the American
Youth Circus Organization (AYCO)
ISBN – 9781733971225
124 pages
MSRP: $15 USD

With over 100 games organized for optimal use in cooperative movement based settings, this is a must have for every circus school, teaching artist, and arts education program! Games are organized by age, number of participants, energy level, and social/emotional learning outcome, and also includes special notes for working with a variety of populations that may require adaptation or modifications to each game. Find more info about the project here:
https://www.americancircuseducators.org/gamesproject/

The ABC Tour

Jon Udry
ISBN – 978-0578410852
MSRP: $25 USD

Ever felt like a challenge? For juggler and comedian, Jon Udry, the ABC Tour — 26 letters, 26 shows — seems the perfect way to shake things up.

What started as a silly idea he believed would take two to three months to complete, ended up being a mammoth three year project that included some of the toughest, most brutal and most enjoyable performances of his life.

From attempting to juggle while wearing roller skates and the unexpected discoveries of performing at a Naturist's Resort, to the challenges that came with working in rainforest conditions covered in ants or in snowy conditions at -10°C, Jon tells the full story from A to Z.

Circus Training Journal

Thom Wall & Rebecca Starr,
Consultant editor: Sarah Baker
ISBN – 978-1-7339712-9-4
9×6" paperback
380 pages
MSRP: $20 USD

What's measured is managed! The *Circus Training Journal* is the result of a year of collaboration between Thom Wall and Rebecca Starr, aerial coach. This undated journal, spanning three months of daily training, tracks workouts, nutrition, goal-setting, and more. Heavyweight paper optimized for ballpoint and pencil.

Artistes of Colour

Steve Ward, PhD
ISBN – 978-1-7339712-7-0
317 pages
MSRP: $25 USD

In a society that places an increasing value in ethnic diversity and cultural identity, the contribution that performers from a variety of ethnic backgrounds made to the development of the circus in the nineteenth century is often dismissed and largely forgotten. Using contemporary records and images, *Artistes of Colour* explores the wealth and depth of talented black and other performers of colour, and their contributions to the success of the nineteenth century circus. Ward draws iconic figures from the margins of history and gives them the recognition they deserve. Long-listed for the American Society for Theatre Research 2022 Book Award.

Contortion and Practices of Body Flexibility in East Asia - Mongolia, China, Japan

Mariam Ala-Rashi
ISBN – 978-1-958604-04-5
MSRP: $25 USD

A collection of three monographs: *China's Bending Bodies: Contortionists and Politics in China; Mongolian Contortion: An Ethnographic Inquiry;* and *The Kakubei Jishi: The Rise, Fall, and Restoration of a Japanese Folk Performing Art.*

This compendium examines contortion and practices of body flexibility in East Asia. It explores the performance art forms Chinese contortion, Mongolian contortion and the Kakubei Jishi lion dance of the Niigata prefecture in Japan which utilizes body flexibility. It discusses the investigation of the history and genesis of these art forms and how they developed in various political and social dynamics. This work further offers vast knowledge about crucial elements such as the artist's training processes, their training environment, the development of aesthetics, symbolism in costuming and body movements, religious themes, mythology and natural phenomena, and costume designs. This compendium includes data from a wide range of literature, material evidence, oral history, current media reports, and considers recent work in anthropology, archaeology, and political history. It offers the interested reader, the scholar, the contortionist and contortion practitioner a substantial treatise about contortionism and practices of body flexibility.

The Contemporary Circus Handbook: A guide to creating, funding, producing, organizing and touring shows for the 21st century

Eric Bates
ISBN – 978-1-958604-03-8
MSRP: $25 USD

The Contemporary Circus Handbook contains interviews with more than 25 professionals, from Gypsy Snider of the celebrated contemporary circus company The Seven Fingers to Lydia Bouchard of La Resistance about their work in the performing arts world. Combining Eric Bates' (Cie Barcode, Cirque du Soleil, et. al.) hard won wisdom as well as tips and insights from his contemporaries, what emerges is an invaluable blueprint of how to progress from the seed of an idea for a show to the full touring timeline. The scope of the book is wide but deeply hands-on, diving into practical details on how to find an agent, start your own company, secure funding and build your niche brand. *The Contemporary Circus Handbook* truly is a unique offering to the circus world, full of insider tips and years of accumulated knowledge from industry insiders.

Opulence & Ostentation

Steve Ward, PhD
ISBN – 978-1-958604-02-1
MSRP: $25 USD

Since the foundation of the 'modern' circus in the eighteenth century, the circus has been presented in defined spaces. Initially, performances were given in the open air and, over a period of time, these spaces first became enclosed and then later roofed. In the nineteenth century, many permanent stone-built buildings were erected solely for the purpose of presenting circus. This phenomenon spread from the UK across Europe and beyond, creating a style of circus architecture that has never been repeated. The purpose of this book is to examine what caused these buildings to be constructed and their design and architecture. Examples of key structures will be explored in detail, some of them still surviving today and still being used for circus performances. The book will also look at the developments of contemporary circus architecture and raise questions as to the future of the circus building.

Cleverer Than God

CLEVERER
THAN
GOD

Erik Åberg
ISBN – 978-1958604113
MSRP: $25 USD

ERIK ÅBERG

Cleverer Than God is a book that tells the story of Paul Cinquevalli, a juggler who rose from the Circus circuit of the 1880s, to attain celebrity status in the British Music Hall and American vaudeville stages until the outbreak of WWI. Through quotes by Cinquevalli himself, woven together with excerpts from journalists and writers of his era, the book tells his story as poignant fragments, capturing the essence of Cinquevalli's triumphs, defining moments, and heart-rending tragedies.

The Juggler's Badge Book

BADGE BOOK

Youth Juggling Academy

Author: Benjamin Domask-Ruh
Editors: Thayer Slichter, Afton Benson
Illustrators: Thayer Slichter and Louis Skaradek
ISBN – 978-1-958604-19-9
MSRP: $25 USD

Introducing *The Juggler's Badge Book*, the ultimate companion for aspiring jugglers! Track your progress, unlock achievements, and earn badges as you learn the art of juggling. With its engaging format and rewarding sticker system, *The Juggler's Badge Book* makes learning to juggle an exciting and fulfilling adventure. Whether you're a beginner or a seasoned juggler, let *The Juggler's Badge Book* be your guide to skillful juggling and a collection of well-earned accomplishments. Start achieving your juggling journey today with this activity book from the Youth Juggling Academy, a program of the International Jugglers' Association!

Published in collaboration between the
International Jugglers' Association and Modern Vaudeville Press.

An International Circus Affair: How a Nanjing Acrobat in San Francisco Changed American Circus Forever

Jeff Raz
Edited by Thom Wall
MSRP: $25 USD
Projected release: Fall 2024

In 1989, the Artistic Director of San Francisco's Pickle Family Circus, Judy Finelli, met briefly with Lu Yi at an airport lounge; Judy now calls it, "A moment that changed circus forever." Lu Yi would move from Nanjing to San Francisco. There he would teach the 2000-year-old art of Chinese acrobatics to the jugglers, clowns, and aerialists of 15-year-old Pickle Family Circus.

This book looks at the 30-years after Lu Yi's arrival in San Francisco and how his acrobatic training and his students' work changed San Francisco and Nanjing – as well as circus around the world, including Cirque du Soleil, The Seven Fingers and many other major circus organizations.

Coming Soon:

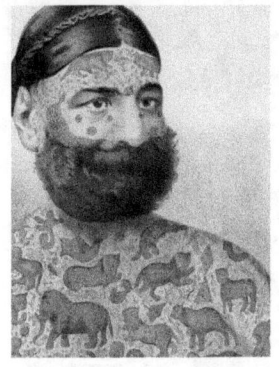

Captain George

Amelia Osterud with Fritz Grobe
MSRP: $25 USD
Coming in 2024!

He appeared out of the blue in Vienna, covered from head to toe in Burmese tattoos. Then, as the Golden Age of American circus began, P. T. Barnum made him the most famous tattooed performer of all time. He said he had been a pirate and a patriot, a rebel and a slave. He claimed he had been tortured by an evil Tatar despot, tattooed by a vengeful sailor in Kashgar, or inked by a princess in Turkistan. Captain George Costentenus told so many outrageous and conflicting tales – what is the truth?

The Century's Juggler

Reinhold Batburger, translated by Kathrin Wagner, edited by Thom Wall
MSRP: $25 USD
Projected release: Winter 2024

He throws a ball in the air and makes millions. And millions of people watch – and did for more than fifty years.

His performance takes seven minutes, and that's his life. Reinhold Batberger tells a family story – the story of a world career, the story of the life and art of juggler Francis Brunn (1922-2004).

Find Our Books Here!

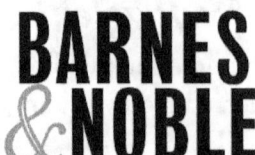

www.ingramcontent.com/pod-product-compliance
Lightning Source LLC
Chambersburg PA
CBHW060924120626
46557CB00003B/867